Law for Project Managers

Law for
Project
Managers

DAVID WRIGHT

GOWER

Published by
Gower Publishing Limited
Gower House
Croft Road
Aldershot
Hants GU11 3HR
England

Gower Publishing Company
Suite 420
101 Cherry Street
Burlington,
VT 05401-4405
USA

David Wright has asserted his right under the Copyright, Designs and Patents Act 1988 to be identified as the author of this work.

British Library Cataloguing in Publication Data
Wright, David
   Law for project managers
   1. Project management - Great Britain 2. Construction
   industry - Law and legislation - Great Britain
   3. Engineering law - Great Britain 4. Contracts - Great
   Britain
   I. Title
   343.4'1078624

   ISBN 0 566 08601 8

Library of Congress Cataloging-in-Publication Data
Wright, David
   Law for project managers / by David Wright.
     p. cm.
   ISBN: 0-566-08601-8
   1. Business law--Great Britain. 2. Project Management--Great Britain. I. Title.
   KD665.B86W75 2004
   346.4107--dc22

                                              2004010172

Typeset by IML Typographers, Birkenhead, Merseyside
Printed in Great Britain by MPG Books Ltd, Bodmin, Cornwall

Contents

Preface

The problem with law is that there is so much of it. Lawyers, politicians and civil servants beaver away in every country of the world making law, year after year after year. In a country like the UK where we have had continuous government since the Norman conquest, they have been doing it for nearly a thousand years, and that has given them an awful lot of time to make an awful lot of law. To make matters worse, some of that law is always going to be complex, obscure and difficult to understand.

Then law and lawyers tend to scare people. When you are dealing both with a subject that is difficult to understand and with a profession that tends to do a poor job of explaining itself to others, this is hardly surprising.

Therefore any book that sets out to explain what the law is and how it works, whether to project managers or anyone else, is giving itself a tough job. Just remember that there are always three stages to understanding how to cope with law:

- Stage 1 – what the law actually is. This is usually not too difficult.
- Stage 2 – what the practical consequences of the law are. This can often be easy; it can also be fiendishly difficult.
- Stage 3 – what the steps to minimise or avoid the problems of Stage 2 are.

That is what this book aims to explain. I hope that I have succeeded.[1]

DAVID WRIGHT

---

1   It should be noted that 'he/his/him' is used as an inclusive pronoun throughout the book at my request.

About the Author

David Wright started out as a contract lawyer in the electrical/electronics/avionic and defence industries. He then spent a number of years as legal manager on the client's side of the off-shore oil industry, and the contracting side of the chemical/process engineering industries. Finally he spent three years at senior management level in charge of the contractual and commercial functions in a UK/communist joint venture process contractor, followed by a period as General Counsel in an mechanical engineering group of companies.

He is now a lecturer and consultant. He is a member of the Institution of Chemical Engineers' (ICHEME) committees which write the Institution's model conditions of contract for the process industry, and which supervise the approval, selection and training of arbitrators and adjudicators. He teaches at a number of universities within the UK on law, contract conditions, negotiation and contract/project management, including Cranfield University, where he holds a Visiting Fellowship in Law, Leeds University and UMIST/Manchester University. He is the author of the *Purple Book*, the standard Guide to the ICHEME conditions of contract and has contributed to two other books. He is an experienced arbitrator, mediator and adjudicator in the process industry.

PART I

General

To understand any system or set of rules properly we have to start by looking at the background and the assumptions that lie behind them.

This is what Chapters 1 and 2 set out to do.

Legal systems throughout the world derive from, or at the very least are influenced by, European legal ideas in their approach to the areas of law that apply to a commercial project. The result is that although virtually every country in the world has its own individual law, there are two common factors that always apply.

The first is that the commercial organisation is expected to be professional, skilled and able to look after its own interests.

The second is that the commercial organisation will get no help from the law if it makes a mistake.

CHAPTER 1

The Law's Approach

This chapter looks at how different legal systems relate to each other, and how the law sees the commercial organisation. The organisation is presumed to be professional, able to look after itself, and therefore has 'freedom of contract', that is, the freedom to drive a hard bargain.

LAW IS ABOUT RELATIONSHIPS

Project managers run projects. Projects deal with getting something done. Projects also involve relationships. Sooner or later every project will involve the project manager in buying in something that is needed for the project from outside the organisation, whether work equipment or services. Once that happens the project becomes dependent on interfaces between organisations – purchaser, contractor, subcontractor/supplier, architect, consulting engineer, quantity surveyor and so on. Some of those interfaces may be informal, but most turn into contracts – and even an informal relationship can actually be a contract whether we know it or not.

As soon as there is a contract the law gets involved. If there is an accident causing injury or damage the law gets involved. If there is an argument over who owns what or who is responsible for doing what, the law gets involved.

Of course most problems or disagreements will be settled by sensible discussion between the parties. When that happens it is useful to know what the law is. Sometimes problems get more serious, and then it becomes vital to know what the law is.

This book aims to give you some of the answers about some of the areas of law that matter most to engineers and project managers running contracts and projects within the UK or under UK law. It helps with other legal systems as well.

LEGAL SYSTEMS

COUNTRIES

In the realms of science fiction we often get a world government. In real life we have to live with something completely different – a world made up of nearly two hundred separate countries, each with its own laws and legal system. It is impossible to describe the law in every country of the world. It is probably almost impossible even to describe the law in any two countries in the world without causing you total confusion.

However there are some common factors. First of all every country has to have law and that law must actually work. If the law doesn't work then everything has to stop until the law is put right. Therefore, however odd the law in any country may look to the outsider, the insider knows that the law will work, and knows how to make it work. When you are involved with a project or contract in another country always remember that local people and organisations will know how their own law works even if you don't. They will expect you to know how it works as well, or at least to know enough to avoid getting into trouble. (And the best source of advice about local law is usually a local organisation, agent, consultant or lawyer.)

Broadly speaking:

- Contract and commercial law is similar in most countries. Even if the theory is different the results will be very much the same; however there may be differences in detail.

- Administrative law, import/export licences, work permits, compulsory insurance and many others will be very different.

- Liability law, compensation for accidents or damage caused to others will be generally similar. Health and safety law will be very similar throughout the European Union, but in other countries may be very different.

- Organisation law, the law of companies and so on may be very different.

- Environmental protection law may vary considerably.

- Criminal law will be different in detail, occasionally very different.

- Intellectual Property law, patents and copyrights and so on will be broadly similar but different in detail.

One or two areas of law are almost identical all over the world, particularly the laws relating to transport/shipping and payment – bills of lading and airwaybills, letters of credit and bills of exchange and so on.

Many of these areas are explored in this book.

FAMILIES OF LEGAL SYSTEMS

Legal systems tend to develop as groups, largely as a result of history. We call these groups 'families' of systems. All the countries within each family have similar, but not identical, law and legal systems.

First there is the Common Law family, systems based on English law. This family includes the UK (except Scotland), the USA, Eire and almost all the countries of the British Commonwealth, plus one or two others. Then comes the Civil Law family, countries whose law goes back in the dim distant past to Roman Law. These include Scotland, the other countries of western Europe and their former empires, and Japan. Then there is the Russian Law family, comprising Russia, China and the countries of East Europe. Finally there are the Sharia Law systems of Muslim countries in the Middle East, Pakistan and elsewhere.

Every country has its own legal system – different courts, judges, advocates and procedures, but the law that they apply is another matter. Common law and civil law often have different theory but usually produce very similar results in commercial areas. Russian law is an amalgamation of common law and civil law ideas. Sharia law systems often borrow ideas from common law or civil law as well, especially in areas of commercial (as opposed to personal) law.

LAW AND COMPANIES

LAW IN GENERAL

In the UK and many other countries law can be very complicated. However remember that there are two kinds of law. There is the law you need to know to avoid trouble. Then there is the law that you need to know to get out of trouble once you're in it. Almost always the law you need to know to avoid trouble is comparatively simple. Once you're in trouble, however, getting out again can be an awful problem.

Every project manager will need help at some time. When we need help we want advice from someone urgently to tell us what the law says we should do. Once we need help it is usually already too late to start looking for the best person to give us the advice we need. It is much better to identify in advance where we can go for help.

LAW PEOPLE AND ORGANISATIONS

The law looks at the world in a very simplistic way. It sees two kinds of people. First there are normal human beings. They are a little weak and helpless, probably not very clever, in legal terms at least, and certainly lacking in commercial bargaining power. As a result they need some protection – as a consumer or as an employee. This has resulted in considerable amounts of protective legislation. Employee protection has been put in place by a number of Acts of Parliament, culminating in the Employment Protection (Consolidation) Act 1978, and then the Employment Rights Act 1996.

Consumer protection comes from a whole mass of legislation, such as the Consumer Protection Act 1987 and the Unfair Contract Terms Act 1977.

Then there is the commercial organisation, which may be of almost any size or type. It can be a single individual, what is known as a 'sole trader'. It may be a partnership, a firm of solicitors or accountants for example, a 'corporation sole' such as a government ministry, a 'corporate aggregate' such as a local authority or the BBC, or a company. (For the sake of simplicity we will call the commercial organisation a 'company' from now on.)

The company is not helpless, even though it may be comparatively small. It is expected to have bargaining power, to understand the law and to employ or buy its skills, be they legal, contractual, technical and anything else. Therefore when it deals it is expected to know what it is doing. If it enters into a contract it does so with its eyes wide open, knowing what its contracts mean and being prepared to take the risks. If it makes a good deal and a good profit as a result, then good luck. If on the other hand it makes a bad deal and loses money, then that is tough. That is freedom of contract. The point is that the law expects the commercial organisation to survive on its own in the cold hard commercial world.

This book is about the law of that cold hard world.

CHAPTER 2

The Contract

This chapter explains the basic principles that make it necessary to get the contract correct. It then suggests some practical rules to assist in doing so.

THE REAL WORLD

When I first started work as a lawyer in the engineering industry I learnt three very surprising facts. Engineers were more interested in carrying out contracts than in reading them; they understood each other better than they understood me; and they preferred to talk to each other rather than to me. The vast majority of contracts still seemed to work out successfully though, despite facts one and two. At first I could not understand why.

We ended Chapter 1 with the statement that in law the world of commercial contracts is a very cold hard world. In real life, most of the time, it is not nearly as bad as that. Companies work well together and often have many contracts with each other over the years. When problems arise they settle them by discussion and without dispute.

Nevertheless there is always the risk that a contract might go wrong, and that discussion between the parties might fail to resolve the problem. When that happens, the better the contract, the safer you are. Therefore this chapter looks at some of the things to remember when putting contracts together.

THE FUNCTION OF THE CONTRACT

Modern economic life is based on contracts. The contract is the only practicable way of creating legal obligations to supply or pay. The contract is the tool that the modern market economy uses to ensure that goods and services can be bought and sold with confidence. If goods and services cannot be bought and sold easily the economy will simply seize up. Therefore commerce and economics demand that the law that governs contracts must be easy, clear and consistent. Furthermore, as the same rules of law have to apply to every contract however large or small, they have to be both general and simple. Law must not get in the way of trade. It is simply there to ensure that commercial promises are kept.

LAW IS SIMPLE, FACTS ARE COMPLEX

English contract law, like all contract law, is therefore very simple, even though it may not look that way. Therefore most of this book is about simple rules. This does not mean that they are always simple to apply. Applying simple rules to complex facts will produce a logical result, but it will not necessarily produce a simple result. Also if the rules look difficult it is because lawyers' logic is different to engineers' logic.

Law only becomes complex or difficult in a few areas. The important areas are:

- the precise rules governing liability (for example, for lateness or for defective equipment or work);

- liability exclusion/limitation clauses;

- contract interpretation (how lawyers manipulate words); and

- the rules and procedures surrounding litigation arbitration and adjudication.

THE BASIC PRINCIPLES

COMPLEXITY

What engineers often fail to realise is just how complex the commercial and technical situation usually is. Look at any contract – the specifications alone will be ten, twenty or a hundred times the length of the contract conditions. Far more disputes arise because of a misunderstanding about the scope of work, specification or service level agreement than about the contract conditions. The problem is not complex law, but complex facts, and people getting the words wrong.

EVERY CONTRACT IS A SEPARATE RELATIONSHIP

In the eyes of the law each contract is its own isolated stand-alone little world – even though the two parties may have had dozens of other similar contracts before. Therefore the terms that have been used in one contract do not apply to another contract, unless they have been specifically written into that contract as well. Very occasionally it is possible to establish that a 'course of dealing' exists. This only occurs when it can be shown that there have already been several previous contracts between the two companies before, *all on virtually identical terms*. In that case it may be possible to imply that terms could be transferable. Outside the worlds of the Stock Exchange, Lloyds, or currency or commodity trading, course of dealing relationships are rare.

Every single contract is an exercise in getting the words right, and not leaving anything out, in case this is the contract that goes wrong.

CONTENT V PROCEDURE

The law is not really concerned with making detailed rules about what conditions must be included in commercial contracts, and does so only where questions of public policy are involved, for instance the outlawing of 'unfair' liability exclusion clauses. Instead it lays down the basic ground rules and then concentrates on mainly procedural matters (such as capacity to contract, how contracts are made and terminated, possible remedies for breach of contract, and so on). The actual provisions of the contract itself are largely left to the parties to decide for themselves.

CONTRACT LIABILITY IS STRICT

A promise under a contract is an absolute responsibility. It doesn't matter that the failure was accidental, due to a subcontractor, or not your fault at all. If you have promised to do something you are liable for any failure to carry out that promise, unless there is a valid legal reason for not doing so. There are only three legal reasons that matter. First is that the contract was frustrated by something that happened during the contract and made it totally impossible (common law), or almost impossible (civil law), to carry out the contract in any way at all. This is rare. The second is that the other party prevented or impeded performance. The third is that there are specific words in the contract that excuse or limit liability for your failure.

Therefore think very carefully about what you promise to do in the contract, and about the words that might protect you if you fail.

A PRACTICAL APPROACH

RULES

Every task becomes easier if we can adopt an organized approach. Here are some possible rules relating to contracts.

Rule 1 – Don't be scared

Far too many engineers shy away from reading contract documents. Maybe they are scared of lawyers. Maybe they are scared of the words. Don't be – read the words and find someone to explain to you anything you don't understand.

Rule 2 – Get the technical parts of the contract correct

For a typical engineering contract the main technical parts of the contract will be the scope of work, the specification and/or the service level agreement, and the test specification. The most important things to do are to:

- clarify the technical situation;

- ensure that the wording of the contract accurately reflects this; and

- ensure that all the different documents interface with each other correctly.

Rule 3 – State clearly what the obligations of each party are

Any project creates dependency risk. For instance the contractor may need information from the purchaser to enable him to design equipment that will interface correctly with other equipment already installed at the site. The purchaser may need information from the contractor about the equipment to prepare the site. The contract should make clear what information each party is to provide to the other and when – and what will happen if the information is late or incorrect, and so on.

What you will not do under the contract is as important as what you will do. Assumptions, qualifications and presumptions at the tendering stage must be dealt with when the contract is put together.

Rule 4 – Say what risks and obligations you will accept and not accept

The comments that we made under Rule 3 apply here also. But there are other considerations as well. Obligation and risk are usually linked in contractual terms. You might be prepared to accept the obligation to deliver against a very tight delivery date, provided that the damages for late delivery (the risk) are set at a low level, for instance.

Rule 5 – Get the timescales right

No comment is needed.

Rule 6 – Check the arithmetic

This sounds simple, but it is astonishing how often we see contracts with elementary mistakes in pricing or quantities.

Rule 7 – Pick a suitable set of contract conditions

This is not the right place to discuss contract conditions in detail. They are worth a book in themselves, or even several books.

As always the basic principle is very easy. Contract conditions lay down a set of rules to enable the parties to carry out their contract. If the contract conditions give the parties rules which are appropriate to the work that is to be done the contract will probably run reasonably smoothly, because the rules will help the parties implement the contract properly. If however the contract conditions lay down the wrong rules, then the rules will get in the way of doing a good job.

Contract conditions are of two different types. First there are in-house conditions, written by one of the parties as a standard basis for its contracts. Second there are model conditions of contract. In-house conditions will always be biased, to a greater or lesser extent, in favour of the company that produces them. Model conditions aim to be reasonably fair to both sides.

Model conditions are generally produced on an industry basis. The Institution of Civil Engineers publishes sets of conditions suitable for civil engineering contracts. The Institutions of Electrical and Mechanical Engineers publish sets of conditions that are suitable for contracts within the electrical and mechanical engineering industries. The Institution of Chemical Engineers publishes sets of conditions that are suitable for contracts in the process industries, and so on. Pick a suitable set of conditions for your contract.

Rule 8 – Read those conditions carefully

Read the contract conditions before contract and ask yourself if they are suitable for what you are going to do. If they are not suitable then ask for changes. If you do not see the conditions until after the contract has been signed then it is too late to change them. But you still need to read them, because they decide a number of important things.

First, conditions often lay down the procedures, how to claim a payment or make a variation for example. Then they allocate responsibility for work or risks. Contract conditions are the relationship rule-book. If you play the contract game according to the rules you are more likely to win than if you don't.

Rule 9 – Check the interfaces

The law requires a contract to be a single document. Of course a complex contract may be made up of many different documents, conditions, specifications, schedules, appendices, attachments and so on. But it is regarded as a single set of promises. Make sure that all the different documents that go to make up the contract interface correctly with one another. If for instance the specification says that the purchaser will provide a particular item of equipment for the project, but the conditions of contract say that the contractor will provide that item then the specification and contract conditions are in conflict with one another. That conflict must be resolved.

The problem is made worse of course by the fact that most contracts are written by several different people. Engineers write the specification. Legal or commercial people write the contract conditions. Insurance provisions may be written by an insurance expert, or shipping conditions by a shipping expert. Then of course the contractor's engineers will write some parts of the specification and the purchaser's engineers will write other parts of the specification. Making sure that all these different people write documents that interface correctly with one another can be a major exercise, but it needs to be done.

Rule 10 – Be consistent

This means getting the terminology right. Terminology is often simply a matter of convention or the jargon of the industry. It can vary from company to company and industry to industry. Some companies use the terms *contractor* and *purchaser*. Others may use *seller* and *supplier* or *vendor* and *buyer*. One company will talk about a *bid*, another a *tender*, and another a *quotation*. One company will use the word *attachment*, another *schedule*, and another *appendix*. Companies talk about *agreements* or *contracts* and so on. The terminology does not matter, provided that it is used consistently throughout the whole document. The law allows the parties to use any terminology.

There are however one or two points to bear in mind. We have already mentioned the problem of potential conflict between the different documents in the contract. However hard we try to eliminate conflict, it is always a risk. One way of trying to minimize this risk is to ensure that if there is a conflict, we know which document will overrule another. We do this by giving the different parts of the contract an order of precedence over each other. Whenever the contract is made up of several different documents it is always a good idea to establish an order of precedence between them.

A typical order of precedence might be:

1. the agreement /contract document itself

2. any special conditions of contract

3. the general conditions of contract

4. the specification

5. any further attachments/schedules and so on

6. any drawings or other ancillary documents also forming part of the contract.

The result would then be that higher-ranking documents would always automatically overrule lower ranking documents should there be any discrepancies between them.

Then we use 'defined terms'. The contract conditions will often start by setting out a list of defined terms, which are to have a particular meaning wherever they appear in the contract. This is a valuable principle but don't get caught out. Say 'EQUIPMENT' is defined as the equipment to be supplied by the contractor, and 'CONTRACTOR'S EQUIPMENT' is defined as meaning the equipment to be used by the contractor on site to install the EQUIPMENT. These terms will then have the same defined meanings, every time they appear in every contract document. EQUIPMENT will be different to

CONTRACTOR'S EQUIPMENT. And 'Contractor's equipment' may even be interpreted in some situations as meaning something different to 'CONTRACTOR'S EQUIPMENT', simply because lower case letters have been used instead of capitals.

Provided we follow these rules the law will then generally take care of itself, provided that:

- you follow the rules of good commercial practice;
- you carry out your side of the contract reasonably to time and specification; and
- you apply those conditions of contract properly.

The last point can be easier said than done. It implies that if you are to manage any contract correctly you do have to know and understand the contract conditions reasonably well. In particular it means that you need to know what rights the different clauses give you and the other party to the contract as well. They will determine how much you can manage and control the other party, especially when things go wrong. This produces one final rule.

Rule 11 – Make sure that you have your sources of contract advice in place in case you need them

No project manager would go into a project without knowing where he would go for specialist advice on the technical side if a difficulty arose. The same principle applies to law and contract conditions. (See Chapter 10.)

The Origins of Law

Every project manager has to live with the law. In the modern world, too, the law that he has to live with is always being updated. It is safe to say that there is always some area of law that is changing. In areas like health and safety, protection of the environment, or control of pollution this process of change and development can at times be very quick.

What Part II does is to explain, in Chapter 3 how the process of making and changing law actually works, and the different roles of the 'Executive', government and civil service, parliament and judges within that process.

Then Chapter 4 describes how the European Union makes law as well, and what functions the different parts of the organisation play.

Law in the UK

> This chapter looks at the different ways in which law is made within the UK, and then examines the practical consequences and problems that this creates.

A SUMMARY

THE LAWMAKERS WITHIN THE UK

Effectively five groups of people have the power to create law:

1. The national assembly – that is Parliament – plus the other national assemblies: the Scottish parliament, the Welsh and Northern Ireland national assemblies, plus the House of Keys in the Isle of Man and so on. All of these assemblies have territorial and other limits to their powers, but within those limits can make law. This is primary legislation – as distinguished from secondary or delegated legislation. It may also be called statute law and will be generally known as an Act of (the Scottish) Parliament for example, as appropriate.

2. Delegated legislation – law made by other bodies to which Parliament has delegated authority to do so. These bodies fall into three groups. Local Authorities are given powers to make laws of various kinds within their own areas. Other bodies may also be given similar powers to control areas of activity, such as the Law Society (solicitors), the BMA (doctors) or the FA (football). All these laws are usually called 'by-laws'. Government departments are often authorised to make laws by particular Acts of Parliament. For example almost all Health and Safety legislation is made this way, by means of 'Regulations' issued by various Ministries under the authority of the Health and Safety at Work Act 1974. These laws are called 'statutory instruments'.

3. Law can be made by judges, by the system known as 'precedent'.

4. Law can be made by the European Union – by a 'Regulation' (see Chapter 4).

5. Finally law can be made by an 'Order of the Privy Council', essentially by government decree. (This would only ever happen in a national emergency.)

LAW MADE BY LEGISLATION

The normal way in which new laws are made in all countries in the world is by legislation, passed by the national assembly/legislature. Even in common law countries like the UK, where law can be made by precedent, the vast majority of new law is made by legislation. In a federal country, such as the USA or Germany (and now the UK), there may be both a national legislature and state legislatures each with their own areas of legislative authority.

Every legislature has its own individual procedure for debating and passing legislation. They are broadly similar in aim, though often very different in practice. All have precisely the same limitations and problems. They are short of time and of skilled manpower. They cannot deal with detail and therefore they have to delegate to others.

THE PROCESS IN THE UK

The process begins with the 'executive' – meaning the relevant government minister supported by his civil servants.

The executive will decide that a new law is required. Once the executive has decided what that law should say, it will have its proposed legislation drawn up in the form of a final draft statute to be submitted to Parliament. This is what we call a 'Bill'. (The word bill simply means a formal document – hence the Bill of Lading, a formal receipt for goods loaded on to a ship.) The bill goes to Parliament. The general procedure is for three readings of the bill in both houses of Parliament, plus a committee stage and finally the royal assent.

Any important bill will begin with a first reading in the House of Commons, followed by a first reading in the House of Lords. (Minor bills may reverse the order, going to the Lords before the Commons.) The first reading simply records the fact that the bill is now on the agenda. Then the bill will receive a second reading, first in the House of Commons followed by the House of Lords. The second reading is a full detailed debate upon the proposals and wording of the bill. Next the bill goes through its committee stage, when a committee of usually between 20 and 50 interested members of the House of Commons examines the detailed text of the bill, clause by clause and line by line, criticising improving and amending the drafting. Finally the bill will go through a third reading in both houses, again the Commons followed by the Lords. The third reading is a short debate on overall principles. Presuming that the bill is voted through at each of these readings it will receive the assent of the Sovereign and become law, changing from a bill to an Act of Parliament.

Obviously it takes a lot of parliamentary time to debate and pass any legislation. The legislative process uses people in vast quantities. Parliament may take several days to debate a bill adequately. The Budget, the annual Finance Act, alone can take up to three weeks. However Parliament, or rather the House of Commons, has many other things to do as well as making laws and only limited time (some 40–45 weeks per year). As a result Parliament can only debate properly some 40 Acts per year. (Of course Parliament may pass many more Acts than that in a parliamentary year, but only by passing them without full debate.)

Also the Commons (like the Lords) is a committee with hundreds of members. It is inefficient. It is not equipped to deal with detail. The most it can do is to deal with broad principles, leaving the detail to others. The method by which this is done is that of delegated legislation.

Many Acts of Parliament therefore include an enabling clause, empowering another body, usually a government department (the executive again) to put in place additional law 'in furtherance of the aims stated in the Act'.

So once the Act is in place the civil servants can move in. Sometimes they may issue literally dozens of statutory instruments under a particular Act. Delegated legislation allows for speed and flexibility and can deal with the detail. It allows the Act to be expanded into detailed sets of rules that can be applied to many different real-life situations. Its disadvantage is that the national assembly loses control to the executive or to local government, which drafts the bill/Act and then writes and issues the delegated legislation. In the UK there are usually some 3–4000 statutory instruments created every year. The number of by-laws created each year is not recorded (but will certainly run into several thousand).

In addition many statutes are also backed up by 'codes of practice'. Sometimes codes may be legally binding – with the status of delegated legislation. More often they are not, with the result that they would then be simply one form of the self-regulation of an industry, or a statement of 'good engineering practice'.

WHAT 'LEGISLATION' MEANS

All this is very well. We have the primary legislation, in England an Act of Parliament. We have secondary legislation, a statutory instrument or a by-law. We can read the text and so we know what they say. If we know what the words say then we must know what the law is. At least that is the theory. In practice however it is not that easy, until the law has been around for some time.

What still has to happen is the third stage of legislation, the interpretation of the legislation by the judges, when the new law begins to be applied to real life situations.

Of course judges do not make law when this happens, but they do explain what it means. In practice there will often be some element of interpretation required and it is the judges who provide that interpretation. Sometimes the judges may even point out that the words of the legislation do not actually mean what parliament intended them to mean at all. The classic example in recent years was the Dangerous Dogs Act, which failed totally in its stated objectives when it reached the courts, and judges in case after case pointed out that the words of the Act were so badly drafted that it was unusable.

Even where the words are clear, guidance may still be required. Consider the following. A new regulation (a statutory instrument) is published under the Health and Safety at Work Act, governing the safety of hand-rails on office staircases. The Regulation states that all employers must take '... *reasonable steps to ensure that hand-rails on staircases are safe for use by employees at all times* ...' A company decides that in order to ensure that the hand-rails on its staircases are safe it is reasonable to inspect and repair (if necessary) the hand-rails once every three months, and, of course, also to repair any other defects as and when reported. After this policy has been in place for a year an accident occurs when an employee is injured due to a defective hand-rail giving way and causing him to fall and suffer a broken ankle.

Investigation shows that the defect in the rail was due to the failure of a bolt that had become loose. The rail was given its three-monthly inspection eleven weeks previously, and the defect in the bolt was not apparent at that time, and had not been reported since. The Health and Safety Executive decide to prosecute the company for an infringement of the new regulation. When the case comes to court the HSE argues that a policy of three-monthly inspection is not 'taking reasonable steps to ensure that the hand-rails are safe'. The company will automatically argue that its inspection policy is reasonable, and that this was simply an unfortunate accident. Once the evidence has been presented the judge will comment on the wording of the regulation in his address to the jury, and the jury will decide whether or not the company is guilty of an offence under the regulation.

Of course the judge will always have to explain what words mean. However in this instance there is also a value judgement to be made. What exactly is reasonable – a 0.0001 per cent risk, a 0.01 per cent risk, a 1.0 per cent risk or a 10.0 per cent risk? Any periodic inspection policy contains some element of risk. Even an hourly inspection contains a minute risk. A daily inspection contains a bigger risk, a weekly or monthly inspection a bigger risk still. Also there is the problem of the staircase itself. Is it steep or not, wide or narrow, well or badly lit, slippery or not and so on. The judge must give the jury some advice on how the value judgement should be made, and the jury cannot help but be influenced by that advice. The moment that this happens the interpretation placed on the words of the regulation by the judge begins to affect the meaning of the law.

It is only now, when we see how the regulation is really being applied, that we can begin to predict what action companies should really take to ensure that the hand-rails on their staircases are safe and that they do comply with the regulation. This process may take months or years. Until that moment everything is guesswork.

Naturally it is not entirely guesswork. Every company can consider 'good industrial practice', or 'best industrial practice', and can make an informed judgement as to what it should do based upon its own experience and on professional advice. Nevertheless until cases begin to come to the courts and the professional lawyers come to grips with the practical application of the words of the legislation to real life situations, nobody can be sure precisely how the law will be applied. And of course the problem for any manager is that he cannot wait that long.

LAW MADE BY JUDGES

In England the judge was seen as the representative of the King. As a result common law systems allow the judges, or at least the higher levels of the judiciary, to make law. It is this that distinguishes the common law systems from others. In the civil law system the judiciary has no authority to make law on its own: it is there to apply the law.

(Of course that is the theory – that under other systems judges do not make law. Their function is simply to apply the law – usually the national code setting out the principles of the law, together with other legislation. But of course the judge still has to interpret the law, and still has to make value judgements in just the same way as a common law judge. And of course judges' decisions are always persuasive to other judges. Once a few eminent judges start applying the law in the same way as each other, other judges will do the same and the bandwagon begins to roll. Therefore under French or German law various areas of law – contract and liability law for instance – have been developed by the judges in very much the same way as in the UK.)

PRECEDENT

The law is made by 'precedent'. This simply means that the decisions made in the upper courts, the Appeal Court and House of Lords, soon perhaps to become the 'Supreme Court', are binding upon lower courts, unless or until overturned or cancelled out by legislation.

Precedent law depends upon three principles:

- reliable Law Reports, so that we know what judges have decided;
- rules for interpreting what a precedent actually decides; and
- rules for deciding which courts can set precedents.

We have had reliable reports on cases since the later part of the nineteenth century. A law report gives the name of the case, a head note that summarises the decision, a brief summary of the legal arguments put by the parties, and the text of the judge's decision. A report of a case can be anything up to 250 pages long (or more). There are now reports on more than 250 000 cases.

In giving a decision the judge will explain his reasons. He will:

- discuss previous decisions;

- say what he finds to be the facts of the case;

- say what he decides that the law is as it applies to the actual facts; and

- discuss what he might have decided upon other facts.

What sets the precedent is the decision of the judge about the law as it applies to the actual facts. Comments upon other possibilities may be persuasive, but cannot bind other judges.

Only the upper courts can create precedents by their decisions. The lower courts, such as Magistrates Courts, the County Court or Tribunals cannot set precedents. The upper courts are:

- The High Court – a judge (or judge and jury in a criminal case) hearing the case at first instance may make a decision on law and fact. Findings on fact will not be open to challenge unless new evidence can be brought forward later (which is only usual in criminal cases, and even then it is rare). The judge's decision on law does not set a precedent, but is persuasive. In other words other high court (and appellate) judges may follow the decision in later cases but do not have to. (There are over 95 high court judges based in London – plus another 150 elsewhere.) Many cases that are regarded as precedents are actually cases decided by High Court Judges, and therefore technically merely persuasive rather than binding. However they have achieved authority by being 'cited', that is, quoted as authoritative by later courts. Appeal against a High Court decision is to the Court of Appeal.

- The Court of Appeal – sits as a court of three. Its judges give separate judgements with a majority decision being decisive. Its decisions set precedents for itself and for all lower courts. (There are about eighteen Lord Justices of Appeal, and another 20 judges who sit in the Appeal Court from time to time.) It hears appeals usually only on law. Appeal against a Court of Appeal decision is to the House of Lords.

- The House of Lords – the highest UK court. Except in very special circumstances it sits as a court of five, with a majority decision being decisive and each judge giving his own judgement. Its decisions set precedents for all lower courts, and it will generally follow its own earlier decisions, though they do not actually bind. (There are about twelve Lords of Appeal, and another three judges, from the Court of Appeal, who sit in the Lords from time to time.) Again it hears appeals usually only on law.

Remember that in the Court of Appeal and the House of Lords there may be three or five quite separate judgements, which may hardly agree at all. Often a complex case will raise several legal issues. Judge A might decide on the basis of a completely different issue to Judge B.

Precedent law is actually quite important to this book, because large areas of commercial law, in particular the law of contract and liability law, (and also company law), were developed by precedent. Judges are actually very good at working out a set of rules – but they are not very good at keeping rules up to date. Legislation is better at keeping up to date.

KEEPING UP TO DATE

We all need to keep up to date, or sooner or later we will be caught out, but there are several problems.

With regard to legislation there is always a problem in finding out what the words will actually mean in practice, until the legislation has been around for long enough for the lawyers and judges to start applying it. With delegated legislation there is an additional problem. Thousands of statutory instruments and By-laws are published every year, and it is extremely difficult, even for the professional, to keep track of all the items that are published.

With precedent the problem is that it can be very difficult both to identify/locate the correct decision and then to interpret what the judges actually decided.

The consequence is that it is very difficult for any company to keep detailed track of changes in law on its own unless it can afford to have a department staffed with experts. Very few companies can afford to do this. Therefore we are all dependent upon others to help us. There are several sources we can use, but the principal ones will be the press, especially professional journals, briefing papers, training courses and so on, and then the sources of advice and assistance referred to in Chapter 10.

CHAPTER 4

European Union Law

This chapter looks at the EU. It explains how it works, what the important bodies within the EU are and how they relate to each other. Finally it examines the different way in which they make law that will apply to companies within member countries.

AN INTRODUCTION TO THE EU

If we are pedantic the European Union was originally made up of three 'communities': the European Coal and Steel Community, the European Atomic Energy Community and the European Economic Community, which adopted common institutions in 1965 and have now merged into one. These communities were created through treaties, the most important being the Treaty of Rome, which set up the EEC. It came into existence in 1957, and the UK joined in 1973. The original number of members was six, current membership is 25, and probably likely to increase to 26. The EU is a confederation of like-minded states which collaborate together for their common good.

THE EU'S POWER TO MAKE LAW

By entering into or acceding to the Treaties all the member-states agreed to transfer some of their law-making powers to the EU for the duration of their membership. The EU is unique. It is the only true supra-national law-making institution in the world. Not even the United Nations can make laws.

THE REASON FOR MAKING LAWS

The EU makes laws to further the objectives agreed by all the member-states when they joined, as set out in the Treaties. The principal objective of the EU is the 'harmonious development of the economic and social activities of member-states'. It does this through various methods, including the fostering of 'undistorted competition', the abolition of obstacles to the free movement of persons, goods and capital, and the 'harmonisation' of the laws (that is, achieving roughly parallel law) of the laws of member-states.

THE ORGANISATION

In law-making terms there are nine important bodies. They are as follows:

THE COUNCIL OF MINISTERS

The Council is a committee, or rather a whole series of separate committees, of government ministers from all the member-states. Various ministers from all the member-governments meet formally in Brussels with their opposite numbers routinely and regularly, at approximately monthly intervals – the Economic Agriculture Home and Foreign ministers especially. Each of these committees, whether agricultural, foreign, or whatever, forms the Council. The Council therefore represents the national governments within the EU. Its principal function is to co-ordinate EU policies, and to provide the prime source of day-by-day political direction. It can also make 'Regulations', approve (that is make) 'Directives' and give 'Decisions'.

The Council has considerable power, because it represents the political element necessary to make law within the member-states.

COREPER

The Council is supported by a 'Committee of Permanent Representatives' or COREPER. COREPER comprises, in fact, the diplomats – senior diplomats of ambassador rank from each member-state with their own support staff (again civil servants and diplomats). COREPER carries out routine administration and prepares for Council meetings. It deals with non-contentious issues (usually at least 50 per cent of the agenda), leaving the Ministers free to concentrate on the contentious or high-profile matters.

Despite its power and political authority the Council is sometimes of only limited effectiveness (and will stay that way until it finally sorts out the problems of majority decision-making). After all, its members are more concerned with running national government. Also as the EU grows, its power tends to become increasingly hard to use. Large committees are always less efficient than small ones, despite the work of COREPER.

THE COMMISSION

The Commission comprises 25 Commissioners, one appointed by each member-state. They are appointed for a five-year period. They head the 'Directorats Generales' within the Commission. They are in fact the heads of large departments, or sub-departments, within the EU civil service, and are backed by dozens or hundreds of high-quality permanent administrative staff. (Never underestimate the EU Commission.) They act independently of the governments that appoint them. They are 'the true Europeans', in that although they are national political appointees, they run the EU.

The Commission has three functions: it administers the operations of the EU; it initiates legislation and it oversees (and virtually polices) the operation of EU law throughout the EU and has considerable enforcement powers. It can impose fines upon individuals/companies for breach of EU rules, and can take offenders before the European Court of Justice (ECJ). Fines for breach of EU law are a very potent weapon. Typical fines fixed by the Commission for a breach of EU law in the area of restrictive trade practices might be anything up to £50 000 *per day*. Fines set by the ECJ are often fixed as a percentage of turnover.

The Commission can make 'Regulations', draw up/propose 'Directives' to the Council of Ministers and give 'Decisions'.

The Commission has enormous influence within the EU because it is at the centre of the communications network between all the various parts of the organisation.

THE EUROPEAN PARLIAMENT

The only elected institution within the EU. It was originally called an Assembly but then began to call itself a parliament and was officially termed a Parliament by the Single European Act of 1986. It began by being almost entirely advisory and in one sense little more than a talking-shop, but with the power to approve the annual Budget (and therefore essentially the operation of the Common Agricultural Policy). Now Parliament must be consulted on all EU legislation and has power to 'suggest' (virtually make), modifications to Regulations and Directives. Its members have the advantage of being permanently within the system. It also has the power to censure the Commission and thereby force the resignation and replacement of the Commissioners.

Like the UK Parliament the European Parliament operates a permanent select committee structure to oversee areas of importance and regularly questions the Commissioners. The Council of Ministers also accepts and answers questions from committees. As with Westminster this select committee system gives the Parliament considerable influence.

Essentially over time the Parliament and the Commission have seen their power and influence over legislation tend to increase whereas that of the Council has tended to decrease. After all, the Council members are government ministers with their own countries to run and only limited time to give to EU matters, while the Commission and the Parliament are permanently at the centre.

THE EUROPEAN COURT OF JUSTICE

(Not to be confused with the Court of Human Rights which sits in the Hague.) The European Court of Justice's (ECJ) jurisdiction includes:

- cases on legal issues arising out of EU law which affect the rights of individuals or companies; and

- matters arising from acts or omissions of member-states companies and individuals involving possible failures to comply with EU obligations.

The court consists of 25 judges, appointed for six years (one from each member-state), and they elect their own president every three years. A quorum for a decision of the *full court* (a plenary session) in a major case is seven judges, and for a decision by a *chamber* either three or five judges, depending upon the importance of the issue. The Court operates very much like a French court. Procedure before the Court consists of three stages: first written submissions, second investigation (questioning witnesses and so on), then oral arguments by the parties. The Court gives a single written decision, which is published in the EU Official Journal.

The ECJ is assisted by an Advocate-General. They investigate each dispute independently but on behalf of the Court, and have powers to interrogate the parties separately from other proceedings and also to attend all hearings. They submit reasoned legal advice to the Court at the end of the oral arguments as to what they might choose to decide. The Court regularly accepts the arguments of the Advocates-General, whose advisory submissions therefore carry great weight. The Advocate General is possibly/usually more expert in the finer points of EU law than the Court itself. Even if the Court refuses to accept the Advocate-General's view, it is still important – as a line of reasoning that the Court has not accepted.

The Court is independent and has jurisdiction over EU institutions, member-states, organisations and individuals on matters of EU law. Its workload has increased enormously as the number of member-countries has increased. This is because the Court also has powers under the Treaty of Rome to give preliminary rulings (guidance) to member-states on cases/matters involving questions of EU law. This is where its *real* power and influence lies – not in the major cases that come before it, but in answering a steady stream of questions from the member-states. The ECJ has a unifying policy. It has always adopted the view that EU law overrules national law (and one that has been accepted without demur by member-states – including the UK). It has also done much to ensure that all member-states accept the same interpretation of EU laws. Each time a new country joins the EU vast areas of its law have to be brought into line with EU law. This means that over a period of some years hundreds or thousands of questions will be referred to the ECJ for decision, each of which will be dealt with by the process described above.

THE COURT OF FIRST INSTANCE

Due to the pressure of work on the ECJ, an additional court came into operation in

1989, the Court of First Instance. There are twelve judges. There are no Advocates-General (but the judges may themselves act in that capacity if they wish). The Court operates in much the same way as the ECJ, and its decisions can be appealed, on law, to the ECJ. It deals with cases involving trade and unfair competition disputes, where there are complex problems of investigating large amounts of factual evidence (which is always an enormous drain upon court time – a serious case could easily involve the judges in reading and dealing with literally several tonnes of documents).

THE ECONOMIC AND SOCIAL COMMITTEE

This is a committee, or rather a consultative/advisory body, of the great and good that acts as a forum for advice on the implications of EU policies. It advises on EU legislation and other matters. Its members are appointed by the member-governments. Its influence is difficult to assess, but quite extensive because it has always allied itself to the Commission. Its members are divided into three equal-sized groups – employers, employees and other interests (that is, pressure groups).

ADVISORY COMMITTEES

In addition the EU operates on the basis of a large number of advisory committees on which all member-states are represented and which meet regularly to advise on the full range of policy matters. The membership of an advisory committee would include representatives of government, industry, pressure groups and so on from all member-countries. Their advice is filtered through the Commission, which provides the secretariat for the committees and is at the centre of the EU's information network. Virtually every aspect of EU policy has at least one advisory committee.

THE EUROPEAN COUNCIL

The European Council, the formal meetings of the Heads of Government in conference, was established in 1974, and has become increasingly important as the deciding body of overall political direction of the EU (witness the Maastricht Treaty and the new EU constitution accepted in Dublin). The European Council was in fact formally created/recognised by the Single European Act. Its operation has reduced the power and importance of the Council of Ministers, since they are no longer the supreme political body within the EU, though they are still the supreme legislative body.

HOW THE EU MAKES LAW

PRIMARY LEGISLATION

There are important differences between the EU and its members. In the member-states new legislation will be made by the national assembly through a law/statute.

This primary legislation may then authorise another body to produce secondary or subsidiary law, which we would then call delegated legislation. (In the UK law may also be made by the decisions of senior judges as we know.)

There is no equivalent system within the EU, because the EU itself does not make primary legislation. It already has what is in effect primary legislation, imposed on it in the shape of the Treaties made or accepted by the member-states (Rome, Maastricht, Amsterdam, the Single European Act and so on).

The EU makes laws in two ways – by means of Regulations and Directives.

REGULATIONS AND HOW THEY WORK

The Treaty of Rome authorised the EU to issue Regulations, to implement policies agreed in the Treaties. A good example of a policy is the Common Agricultural Policy.

Regulations may be issued, either by the Council of Ministers or by the Commission. There are four different detailed procedures that can be followed. All four involve a complex series of preliminary consultations with the European Parliament, the Economic Social Committee, the relevant advisory committees and member-governments on the content and wording of the Regulation. Once this is agreed the Regulation is drawn up by lawyers within the Commission in all the different languages and then signed by the President of the Commission or the President of the Council of Ministers. It is then published in the Official Journal. Regulations are usually immediately binding throughout the member-states of the Community 20 days after publication, unless a longer adjustment period is allowed. This is why so much consultation is necessary. Brussels has to make sure that the Regulation is acceptable to the member-states and will work before it is signed and published.

A Regulation is, in effect, subsidiary legislation made under the authority of a Treaty. It is drafted by lawyers and reads like all legislation.

The vast majority of the Regulations issued by the EU, which run to an average annual total approaching five thousand, relate to administrative decisions necessary to update the Common Agricultural Policy. There are however a number of significant Regulations regulating trading conditions within the Community and the Regulation route is used in other areas, such as restrictive trade practices, use of patents and know-how, trading standards and social policy. There are also many significant Regulations in place dealing with working conditions, health and safety, and environmental protection.

DIRECTIVES AND HOW THEY WORK

Right from the start it was recognised that it was impossible for the Treaty of Rome or for any other treaties to cover all possible eventualities. The Treaty of Rome therefore provided an additional legislative route to enable member states to make additional EU law outside the areas covered by the treaties, where member states thought that it would be a good idea to do so. The prescribed route is that of the Directive; they are used essentially for two main purposes.

First they have been used to harmonise national laws within the EU. A good example of this is that of company law. It was recognised that every member-state within the EU had its own company law, and that every state had different company law. It was also recognised that these differences presented problems. Therefore during the 1970s the EU put in place a series of Directives with regard to the harmonisation of company law. For instance the first company law Directive dealt with the problem of differences in the laws regulating the amount of information to be provided in the annual accounts of public companies. It provided that every member-state should require public companies to publish the same minimum amount of information. (What the Directive actually did was to require every country within the EU to legislate for corporate accounts which contain almost exactly the information required under the Companies Acts in the UK. It imposed English law in this area on the whole of the EU.)

The other area where Directives are used is where it is generally recognised that some change to existing law is a 'good thing' which needs to happen within the EU. The classic example of this is the creation of a law of product liability throughout the EU, which was done by the Product Liability Directive, No. 85/374/EEC. This had an investigation period running from 1973 to 1984, one of the longest ever, and was issued in July 1985. It was then implemented in the UK by the Consumer Protection Act in 1987, and came into force 1987–88. In contrast a Directive relating to compulsory competitive tendering for major public contracts was published within two years of the initial approaches by the Commission to the Parliament, and less than six months after the publication of a draft by the Commission.

Only a few Directives require a statute to implement them. Most are dealt with through secondary legislation. For instance many engineers will know the Construction (Design and Management) Regulations (1994) which lays down minimum design and safety requirements on construction sites within the UK. This is actually a statutory instrument, No. 3010 dated 10 December 1994, issued under the Health and Safety at Work Act, which implements EU Directive, No. 92/57/EEC.

The procedure for making a Directive is that the Commission is responsible for investigating the possibilities and then preparing a draft Directive for consideration by the Council of Ministers. The first stage of investigation usually involves two things: first researching the current position throughout the EU, and then consultation to identify the various possible ways of achieving the desired objective. The second stage involves drawing up draft proposals and discussing those draft proposals with all interested parties. The interested parties include the Economic Social Committee, the European Parliament, member-governments and any interested parties or organisations within member-states. Once a proposal for a Directive is broadly agreed the Commission draws up a draft proposal, in other words a draft Directive, and submits it to the Council of Ministers for approval. By this time of course approval by the Council of Ministers, while not purely a formality, is extremely likely.

Once approved by the Council of Ministers the Directive is published in the Official Journal of the EU and becomes effective. It is in the form of an instruction to all member governments to make whatever changes are necessary to their own national law to ensure that it complies with the requirements set out in the Directive. The method by which law is to be changed is left to member governments to decide. The Directive also sets a time period within which member governments are to comply. The usual period for compliance will be at least two to three years, unless during the consultation period member governments have agreed to a shorter period of time. Finally the Directive will usually require the Commission to liaise with member governments and report back to the Council of Ministers on the progress in passing the necessary national legislation.

WHAT ARE THE DIFFERENCES BETWEEN A REGULATION AND A DIRECTIVE?

The contrasts between a Regulation and a Directive are reasonably clear:

- A Regulation is directly applicable and is immediate law in all member states of the Community without any further action being required. A Directive on the other hand instructs governments to change law. The result is that there may be considerable delays before that change becomes effective. It also results in national legislation, but national legislation resulting from political direction by the Council of Ministers.

- A Regulation is delegated legislation issued by the Commission or the Council of Ministers, under a Treaty and is immediately binding. A Directive is an instruction issued to member-governments by the Council of Ministers, acting with the authority of the Treaty behind them.

The similarities between the two are equally important:

- Both are drafted by the Commission, which therefore has a pivotal role in the legislative process of the Community.

- Both are drafted by lawyers as legal/legislative documents, with a high degree of drafting skill involved in the way they are written.

- Both depend upon a considerable degree of consultation within Brussels and with outside bodies.

DECISIONS AND HOW THEY WORK

Finally we have to mention the Decision. A Decision does not make law, but it tells us what the law is. The Decision is binding upon the parties affected by that Decision, but it also explains to everyone else within the EU how the law would apply to them if they were in the same position. Decisions can come from three sources: the ECJ, the Commission and the Council of Ministers.

Any decision by the ECJ whether in a case before the court or regarding any other matter submitted to the ECJ for advice by any member government or any court in a member state declares what the EU law is on that point. All decisions by the ECJ are published in the Official Journal.

In addition any organisation or person within the EU is entitled to apply for advice on any question relating to EU law to the Council of Ministers or the Commission (usually the Commission).

For example two companies intend to enter into a patent/know-how and product distribution agreement. They are concerned that the proposed agreement might infringe the EU law on freedom of cross-border trade within the EU. They can apply for advice on whether their proposed arrangement is acceptable under EU law to the Restrictive Trade Practices Directorate within the Commission. The Directorate will consider the matter (and if necessary consult the ECJ), and will then give the parties its formal Decision whether or not the proposed arrangement complies with EU law. In addition the Directorate will also give the parties the benefit of its advice. If its Decision is that the proposed arrangement infringes EU law, the Directorate would usually advise the parties as to how to modify their arrangement in order to comply with the law.

The Decision will be published in the Official Journal.

THE OFFICIAL JOURNAL

Current sections of the Official Journal are available on-line or can be purchased. Current and back issues are usually available in the commercial section of major central public libraries.

PART III

Contract Law

Commerce needs contracts to work in much the same way all over the world – Birmingham or Beijing, Brussels or Brasilia, it makes no difference. Whatever the legal theory the practical results have to be much the same. Consumer protection law can vary from one country to another, but commercial contracts *must* work in the same way.

Of course detail may be different. For example some countries permit clauses in commercial contracts that exclude consequential liability, (the UK or Germany), while others only permit clauses that limit consequential liability (France or Portugal). Some countries insist upon various kinds of compulsory insurance cover or operating licences, while others do not. Nevertheless the overall principle holds good.

Part III sets out the rules that apply to the commercial contract.

Chapter 5 deals with how the contract is made and how the commercial organisation uses agents to act on its behalf, while Chapter 6 explains the law relating to the 'letter of intent/instruction to proceed'.

Chapters 7 to 9 then deal with the difficult areas: how the law will decide what the words of the contract actually mean if there is any disagreement between the parties, responsibility for performing the contract, and what we are entitled to if the other side breaks their word.

How Contracts are Made

This chapter explains the Offer and Acceptance process by setting out the rules and then applying them to a practical example. It then looks at the law of Agency, which decides who can act on behalf of the organisation.

INTRODUCTION

THE CONTRACT

The contract is a set of promises between the parties that the law will enforce.

Not all promises make contracts. In our personal lives we make promises all the time, but we do not intend most of those promises to be binding. Personal promises therefore, such as a promise to share a car on a trip to an away football match, are not enforceable unless it is absolutely clear that the parties intended them to be.

Commercial promises, on the other hand, are made in the context of business. The law expects the company to intend its promises to be binding. Therefore promises made by the company will normally be enforceable, provided the other requirements for a contract are satisfied, unless it is absolutely clear that they are not meant to be binding.

WHY ARE CONTRACTS ENFORCEABLE?

In English law the contract is a bargain. In a bargain each party gives something to the other and gets something in return. The fact that the promises are mutual and made in respect of one another creates a contract. The bargain should be kept. Therefore the contract should be carried out. This principle applies in all common law countries.

Under civil law we have a totally different approach. Civil law operates on the basis of a general theory of 'obligation'. Under this theory I have many obligations to other people in society. I have obligations not to commit a crime or to cause an injury by being negligent. In just the same way I have an obligation to carry out a promise to someone else, if that promise has been made deliberately and with serious intent.

These two theories are totally different. However take a practical example, say a contract to buy a computer for £5000.

In England the contractor promises the purchaser to deliver the computer, and the purchaser promises the contractor to pay the £5000. The exchange of promises creates a bargain, and therefore a legally binding contract.

In France the theory is totally different. When the contractor promises to deliver the computer, that is a promise made deliberately and with serious intent. Therefore it is binding. When the purchaser promises to pay £5000 that is also a promise made deliberately and with serious intent. Therefore it is binding as well. (And the fact that each promise is made in return for the other will help the French judge to decide that the promises were made deliberately and with serious intent.) Different theories – identical result.

THE REQUIREMENTS FOR A CONTRACT

In the UK and in other common law countries we need:

- Capacity

- Intent

- Certainty of terms

- Consideration

- Legality of purpose

- It must be possible to identify the terms of the contract and the moment when the contract was made by applying the rules of 'Offer and Acceptance'.

In civil law and other non-common law countries there is normally no requirement for consideration. The only other difference is in the details of capacity law.

CAPACITY

The parties to the contract must have the power/ability to make that contract. There may be many reasons why people do not have the capacity to make a contract. They may be bankrupt or in prison for instance. Companies however, since the Companies Act of 1989, are automatically presumed to have the power to make any normal trading contract that they have actually made. The same is true of other commercial organisations.

However when dealing with companies or other organisations outside the UK, or with unusual contracts, it is always worth checking whether the company or organisation has the capacity to make the contract, and also who has the authority to sign the contract (see Agency, p. 47). Sometimes, for example, companies have to be licensed to carry out certain types of work (see Legality below).

INTENT

The law presumes that the commercial company intends its promises to be contractually binding, unless it is absolutely clear that no contract was intended. But, as a judge said over a hundred years ago 'the devil himself knows not the mind of man'. Every legal system talks about 'the intention of the parties' but no-one can ever prove what anyone really intends. Therefore the law operates not on the basis of real intention, but on the basis of presumed intention. The principle is not whether you intended to make a contract, but whether a reasonable person would have thought that you intended to make a contract. In other words if the company has acted as though it intended to make a contract, by going through what appears to be an Offer/Acceptance process, then the company did intend to make the contract (even if it didn't).

CERTAINTY

In a commercial situation until the parties have agreed *all* the terms of the contract in reasonable detail, there is no contract. The parties will be deemed to be still negotiating. People often make the mistake of thinking a deal has been struck although some points are still to be agreed (see below and Chapter 6).

The law will often imply terms into a consumer contract to help deal with uncertainty in its terms, but it is rare for this to happen in a commercial contract (see the section on Implied Terms in Chapter 7 below).

CONSIDERATION

Consideration is lawyer's jargon for the bargain element necessary for contracts under English law. If we make a bargain, then I give you or promise to give you something that has some value (however small), and you give me or promise to give me something in return that also has a value (however small). What I give you is consideration for what you give me, and vice versa. If we each give the other or promise to give the other something then we have made a bargain; that bargain becomes a contract, and that contract is legally enforceable by both sides, even if the consideration is not of equal value.

DOES CONSIDERATION HAVE TO BE OF EQUAL VALUE?

In law it has to have some value but that is all. A contract to sell a diamond for 10p would be binding, even if the diamond was worth £1 million.

LEGALITY

A contract to carry out an act that is contrary to law, or that can *only* be carried out by acting in an illegal way will be illegal. It will therefore have no legal effect.

OFFER AND ACCEPTANCE

The mechanism used by English/common law to decide whether a contract has been made is that of offer and acceptance. This means, simply, that for a contract to exist one party has to offer the terms and the other party then has consciously to accept that offer.

The idea is almost universal. Civil law systems use different language, but apply the same principles. A French or German judge would follow the same line of reasoning as an English judge.

OFFER AND ACCEPTANCE

The Offer and Acceptance process is simple in outline but needs a detailed explanation to understand how it operates in practice. To see how the process works we will take a typical practical example, set out the rules, and then examine how they would apply to the example.

Example

- Step 1 – the purchaser talks to the contractor about the possibility of placing a contract for some work.

- Step 2 – the purchaser sends to the contractor a written enquiry for the contract. The enquiry describes the work and is on the purchaser's standard enquiry paperwork, with small-print 'terms and conditions of purchase' on the back.

- Step 3 – the contractor raises various questions concerning the enquiry with the purchaser who answers them. The purchaser also raises various questions with the contractor, which the contractor replies to in turn.

- Step 4 – the contractor sends an e-mail to the purchaser stating a price for carrying out the work. In the e-mail the contractor states 'We are broadly in agreement with the terms set out in your enquiry but there are a number of matters which we would like to discuss further with you before we accept a contract.'

- Step 5 – the purchaser and contractor negotiate with each other on the basis of the email by the contractor but do not reach final agreement.

- Step 6 – the contractor now submits a Tender to the purchaser for the work, in accordance with the original Enquiry and the various points agreed during

Steps 3 and 5 and without the qualification referred to in Step 4. The Tender is on the contractor's standard sales paperwork, with small-print 'terms and conditions of sale' on the back.

- Step 7 – the purchaser responds to the contractor's Tender by asking for a reduction in price of £500, and that his conditions of purchase should apply.

- Step 8 – the purchaser issues a 'Letter of Intent' to the contractor on the basis of which the contractor begins the work.

- Step 9 – the contractor responds to the purchaser's request in Step 7 by offering a price reduction of £250, and agreeing the change to the conditions of contract.

- Step 10 – the purchaser issues a purchase order to the contractor at the price stated in Step 9.

- Step 11 – the contractor accepts the purchase order issued under Step 10, by e-mail and a few days later by letter.

The Rules

Rule 1 – Offers can be made and accepted by either side
It makes no difference. The purchaser can make an Offer which the contractor accepts – *or* the contractor can make an Offer which the purchaser accepts.

Rule 2 – Offers can be made verbally or in writing
After all an Offer made over the telephone, by e-mail, or across the negotiating table has to be just as good as one that is written down.

Rule 3 – An Offer has to be complete
To qualify as an Offer all the following items must be adequately covered:

- Specification and scope of work (description of the equipment/work to be supplied)

- Price or price calculation basis (a schedule of rates or bill of quantities is one example of a price calculation basis), and terms of payment

- Conditions of Contract (and time-scale)

- Open for acceptance

- Within a validity period.

Rule 4 – The Offer must be 'unconditional'
Any Offer that states that any item within it is incomplete or still subject to further discussion, or that acceptance of it is 'subject to confirmation' for instance is not an Offer, but a 'Budget Offer' (see below).

Rule 5 – There cannot be a contract until one party has made a complete Offer to the other

Because the contract is made by Acceptance of an Offer.

Notes:

1. The rules set out above are correct for normal commercial contracts. They are not correct for all contracts. There will always be odd situations in which the courts will say that an offer has been made, and accepted, in order to find a solution to a problem. However these odd situations do not concern us.

2. The consequences of these five rules are that preliminary documents and communications have no contractual effect:
    - The normal enquiry, requesting prices and so on from contractors for supplying equipment or work, is not an Offer but, in lawyers' jargon, an 'Invitation to Treat', that is an invitation to negotiate. It therefore does not create any obligation – unless and until the words in the enquiry become part of a contract.
    - The 'budget offer', an Offer giving a 'budget price', or 'subject to further discussion' or that, for instance, stated that certain items still have to be priced, is still provisional or incomplete. Therefore it is not an Offer, even though it may be a very important part of the negotiating process. It is simply a further Invitation to Treat.
    - Other preliminary communications are similar.

Rule 6 – An Offer will cease if it is rejected by the other party or when its 'validity period' ends

Rule 7 – Under English law some Offers can be withdrawn during their validity period

---

Notes:

3. The result of Rule 6 is as follows:
    - If an Offer is rejected by the other side it ceases to exist. I cannot reject an Offer today and then try to accept it tomorrow. All I can do is to ask you to bring it back to life, or offer the same terms back to you and hope that you will accept them.
    - Most commercial offers are given a fixed validity period, 'open for acceptance for 30 days' for example. An Offer with a fixed validity period ceases to exist at the end of that period. An Offer without a

> fixed validity period will be valid for 'a reasonable period', which will depend on the circumstances.
> 4. Rule 7 is an oddity of English law. Most other legal systems do not allow this. But under English law I can withdraw an Offer at any time during its validity period, except where:
>   – The Offer was made under seal, or 'as a deed', that is with the company seal on it, or
>   – There was consideration for the Offer, for example 'If I pay you £20 will you guarantee to keep the Offer open until XXXXXX'.
>   – Of course if the Offer has been accepted it is too late to withdraw.

Rule 8 – A Counter-offer rejects the previous Offer but makes a new Offer instead

Most commercial contracts are made by an enquiry, some negotiation, an Offer, several Counter-offers as the parties negotiate, then finally an Acceptance of the last Counter-offer.

Rule 9 – An Offer can be accepted in many different ways

By any action that demonstrates agreement, or by any statement of Acceptance verbally (either direct or by telephone), in writing, by letter, telex, fax, e-mail and so on. The act must imply acceptance, the statement must confirm acceptance.

Rule 10 – Acceptance must be made by the person to whom the Offer was made

Or by someone acting on his behalf.

Rule 11 – Acceptance must be communicated to the person who made the Offer

Because if we don't know that an Offer has been accepted, and a contract made, we must be free to sell the goods or services to somebody else.

Rule 12 – The Offer can only be accepted in full

Partial acceptance of an Offer will usually be a Counter-offer.

Rule 13 – Acceptance turns the Offer into a contract

A situation once occurred in which two companies sent each other identical offers, one to buy goods at a price and the other to sell the same goods at the same price. The letters crossed in the post. Then one company changed its mind. The judge decided that there was no contract. The Offers showed that both parties were willing to make a deal, but they did not *actually* make the deal.

Rule 14 – Communication of Offers and Acceptances must be done properly

The most important rules on the communication of Offers and Acceptances are as follows:

- Acceptances made by letter are valid from the moment they are posted, not from when they are received.

- All Offers and Acceptances made by any other method – oral, telephone, telex, e-mail and so on – are valid from the moment they are received.

- Acceptance of an Offer can be made either by a statement of acceptance or by actions known to the other party showing that the Offer has been accepted – inaction or silence cannot constitute Acceptance (except in theory).

- If an Offer names a particular method(s) of Acceptance, then other methods of Acceptance will be invalid.

- A withdrawal of an Offer by letter or any other means is valid only from the time that it is received.

If therefore, for example:

DAY 1   You receive an Offer.
DAY 7   The other party posts a letter to you withdrawing the Offer.
DAY 8   You post a letter accepting the Offer.
DAY 9   You receive the withdrawal letter.
DAY 10   The other party receives your acceptance letter.

. . . you would have a contract.

The Example – revisited

Now let us return to the example set out on pages 40–41 above and see how the rules may be applied to the facts.

Step	Interpretation	Rules applying
1	Starts the process, but does not create any liability or commitment on either side.	3 – 5
2	An Invitation to Treat – see note 2.	3 – 5
3	A vital part of the process, but no liability or commitment.	3 – 5
4	An e-mail is certainly a valid contractual communication. The only question is whether it is classified as verbal or written communication under Rule 2. In this example the point doesn't matter, but see below. Step 4 is a budget offer, since the contractor has stated that he wishes to have further discussion of various points before contract.	2 – 5

Step	Interpretation	Rules applying
5	As Step 3. Even though agreement is now near, and the parties are getting close to an agreement there is still no liability or commitment whatsoever.	3 – 5
6	Step 6 is an Offer. It includes specification and scope of work, drawn from the original Enquiry document and the negotiations during Steps 3 and 5. It also contains the price from Step 4, and finally is based upon a set of conditions of contract, comprising the small print terms and conditions on the reverse of the contractor's standard paperwork. Now, and only now, in accordance with Rules 3 to 5, can the Offer and Acceptance process finally begin.	1 – 5
7	A Counter-offer. The purchaser has rejected the contractor's offer at Step 6 and made a new offer comprising the same specification and scope of work, but a lower price and a different set of conditions of contract.	6 and 8
8	See Chapter 6 below. The point however is that there is more than one way of creating liability responsibility and commitment. Probably the purchaser cannot afford to wait too long before work on his project commences. Going through a lengthy Tender/Offer/Acceptance process can take weeks or months, and sometimes projects cannot wait that long. Therefore the purchaser has used a Letter of Intent to get work started before the contract is actually in place.	
9	A second Counter-offer. The change is only comparatively small, an increase in the price on the previous offer of £250, but it is still a change.	6 and 8
10	The purchase order now accepts the Offer made by the contractor in Step 9 in full. Contractually therefore Step 10 will be the Acceptance that creates the contract.	9 – 14
11	In the circumstances, in purely contractual terms Step 11 may be completely unnecessary. The contract has already been made by Step 10. However commercially it may be important for formal acceptance of the purchase order to be issued.	9
	If, however, the circumstances were different and the purchase order had made a change to the terms offered by the contractor in Step 9, then Step 10 would not have been an acceptance (and contract), but merely another counter-offer. In that case Step 11 would have accepted the purchase order, and the e-mail acceptance would probably have been the date of the contract. The final confirmation letter would have merely given formal confirmation.	9 – 14

THE 'BATTLE OF THE FORMS'

This is a problem that often occurs in standard purchasing operations. Typically it happens as follows. The purchaser sends out an enquiry that is subject to his own standard conditions of purchase. The contractor submits an offer that is subject to the contractor's standard conditions of sale. The purchaser then places an order subject to his standard conditions of purchase and the contractor acknowledges that order subject to his standard conditions of sale. In other words each party responds to the other by simply reinstating his own requirements.

In this position the law is simple – there has to be a winner. It is up to the parties to decide which of these two conflicting sets of requirements will apply. The winner will be the party that is the last to assert or insist upon his own conditions before the contract actually commences. In other words in the situation set out above if the purchaser now simply accepts the situation, by for example paying the down-payment, issuing instructions or drawings (in other words accepting the contractor's last Counter-offer), then the contract will be governed by the contractor's conditions of sale. If however the purchaser then objects to the contractor's conditions and re-demands his own conditions then it is for the contractor to decide whether to accept or not.

PUTTING IT IN WRITING

VERBAL CONTRACTS AND WRITTEN CONTRACTS

It is far better if commercial contracts are in writing rather than merely verbal. In principle there is no difference between a contract made in writing, by a formal contract document or by an exchange of documents, and a contract made orally by a face-to-face agreement or a telephone conversation. However there is an enormous practical difference between them. When a contract is made in writing there is no difficulty in proving the exact terms of the contract. When a contract is made orally there is much more room for argument later because there is no immediate direct proof of what was actually agreed.

IS AN E-MAIL (OR A FACSIMILE) VALID IN LAW?

They are valid in law – provided that you can prove (if necessary), what the text was that was sent and that it reached the company to whom it was sent.

IS AN E-MAIL 'WRITING' OR A 'VERBAL' COMMUNICATION?

Basically writing is marks on a piece of paper. Any handwritten or typewritten/printed document, provided it is properly identified/signed and dated, is a written document. A drawing is, or can be, a written document. So also is a telex or a facsimile (provided it is sent to a fax machine), but remember that what matters is what reaches the recipient not what is transmitted. Mistakes in transmission are universally the risk of the sender.

At the moment the EU is busy legislating for e-commerce. The Electronic Communications Act 2000 has already allowed for the legality of 'electronic signatures' and therefore e-commerce, and e-mail is now beginning to assume the status of writing. However most major companies perhaps still feel that e-mail and other forms of electronic communication should not properly be treated as a written document unless secure e-mail software is in place. Secure software automatically identifies any changes made to the text of any e-mail after it has been sent. And of course it is perfectly possible, at least in theory, to interrogate a hard disc and identify precisely what message was sent and received. Perhaps the correct policy is to treat e-mail as written communication, but to make provision in the contract as to how e-mail messages are to be logged and preserved. A typical method is to ensure that messages should be preserved by being automatically copied to a separate tamper-proof file.

A DEED

Any written contract can be made in two different ways: either as a normal signed contract; or as a 'contract signed as a deed' or under the company seal. The only practical difference between the two is that if you are in breach of a signed contract, litigation or arbitration can be started within six years after the contract was completed. If the contract is signed as a deed, litigation or arbitration can be started within 12 years after completion. Obviously this difference is not of any major importance in most contracts relating to equipment. However it can be of some importance in cases relating to civil engineering or building contracts.

A deed is binding not because it is a contract, but because of the way it has been made. A promise to pay money made as a deed, for example, would be binding even if there is no consideration for the promise.

AGENCY

Like many areas of law, agency looks complicated but is not difficult to deal with if we follow a few simple principles.

SIGNING CONTRACTS

A Sole Trader

The sole trader can sign a contract, together with anyone else authorised to do so as his agent.

A firm

Any partner in a 'firm' can sign a contract, and any employee of the firm authorised to do so as an agent. Often large firms will have an internal policy under which only a small number of the partners can sign contracts for the partnership.

A Corporation

The head of a corporation can sign a contract and anyone else authorised to do so as an agent.

A Company

Anyone authorised as an agent can sign a contract for a company.

THE AGENT'S FUNCTION

The function of the agent, in terms of the contract, is to act on behalf of a principal. The agent can do this both when the contract is being made, and during the life of the contract. His actions commit the principal, though he himself will not normally incur any responsibility. In other words, when the agent agrees the contract, the principal is bound by it.

WHAT IS A CORPORATION?

A corporation is a body created by statute, and headed by a person or a group of persons. Legally every contract with the corporation is a contract with the head of the corporation, or the group, whoever they happen to be at the time. Every time a person changes, the contract moves on to the new person. As an example think of a contract with a government department, such as the Department of Transport. Every time there is a new Minister of Transport the contract switches to him or her. And of course the minister cannot sign every contract.

WHAT IS A COMPANY?

A company is a 'legal person' owned by, but separate from, its shareholders. In other words it exists in law, but in no other way. It is not like a human being. A human being can make his/her own contracts but the company cannot do so. It cannot talk and it cannot sign an agreement itself. It cannot do anything itself. It can only act when an agent acts on its behalf.

THE RULES OF AGENCY

It is important to understand the rules. They decide when an employee or director is entitled as agent for the company, and what powers he has when he does act as agent.

This is one area where there is a serious difference between *both* theory *and* practice in common law and civil law systems. Common law systems usually work on the theory that the agent will have *full* powers to act on behalf of his principal within his area of authority. Civil law systems operate on the opposite theory, that the agent will have *only* the powers and area of authority specifically granted to him. Therefore the only safe course when dealing with organisations outside the UK, if in any doubt, is to check that the contract is being signed by someone with real authority to do so.

The English law rules are as follows.

Authority

There are three different kinds of authority:

- 'Express' or 'actual' authority is the authority actually given by the company to the agent. For example, 'As Sales Manager you have the authority to sign contracts, provided that the price is not more than £X000. Board approval is required above that level.'

- 'Implied' authority is the 'normal' authority that anyone would expect that person to have. You would always expect the sales manager to have the authority to sign a sales contract, whatever the size.

- 'Apparent' or 'ostensible' authority is the authority that the other side is reasonably entitled to think that you have, whether you have it or not.

Agents

The usual agents of the company are its employees. In very broad terms, there are three categories of agent within the employees of any company. These are as follows:

1. Most British companies have Articles of Association that are in line with the standard forms laid down in the Companies Acts. These standard Articles empower the board of directors, as a group, to make all decisions and contracts on behalf of the company. Therefore the board has actual authority to act as agent on behalf of the company.

   In addition many companies have Articles that include additional specific powers. A typical example would be an Article giving the managing director of the company the (actual) authority to make trading contracts on behalf of the company. This means that any contract that is a part of the trading activities of the company is valid if signed by the managing director.

   The Board is then entitled to delegate authority to any other person to make contracts on its behalf. This will normally be done in two ways: by giving express authority in specific cases, or by giving managerial (implied) authority, to someone.

2. Therefore the next level of authority within the company is that of executive directors, departmental managers and senior deputies within any department. Here the rule is that where the board gives to any person the power/responsibility to manage any part of the company's operations then that person will have the implied authority to make any contracts as agent for the company within his area of managerial responsibility. In other words any

sales contract signed by the sales director or sales manager will automatically bind the company because it is signed by the person who has the authority to manage the sales activity. Equally any purchasing contract signed by the purchasing director, the purchasing manager or deputy managers within the purchasing department will be binding on the company, because it is signed by a person with managerial authority in that function.

3.   The third level of authority is that of apparent/ostensible authority. The principle is simple, but needs to be thought through. If the company either:
   – puts one of its employees into a position in which that employee appears to have the authority to make a contract, or
   – allows one of its employees to act as though he has the authority to make a contract, or
   – to do anything else of contractual significance;

   and it is reasonable for the other side to assume that the employee did have the authority to do what he did; then the employee is an agent for the company and what he does binds the company.

Note that the contract will bind the company even if the employee did not have any authority, or exceeded the actual authority that he had been given by the company. The reason for this is quite simple. The law looks at two parties: first the company that put the employee into that negotiating position, or allowed the employee to put himself into that negotiating position; and second the other side. If there is a dispute one party has to lose. The law takes the simple position that the company should make sure that its own employees act properly. It is not the responsibility of the other side to make sure that someone else's employees behave properly.

If, for instance, you send one of your assistants to a meeting to discuss the price for carrying out a contract variation and he agrees a price for that variation, the other side would be reasonably entitled to think that he has the authority to do so – because he came to the meeting. As a result you would be bound by the agreement even if it was not what you wanted.

Subject to confirmation

Most contracts will be made by agents operating correctly, and within their level of authority. However it will sometimes be the case that you will agree a deal with the other side even though you have found it necessary to go beyond your authority level in order to do so. In that case there are two alternative situations. If you do not tell the other side that the deal is outside your actual authority, the deal will bind the company on the basis of your apparent authority. Alternatively, you can tell the other side that you need to get management approval for the deal. Your company will then have the choice of either ratifying the deal that has been made or of refusing to accept it. The words to use might be 'Subject to confirmation by ... I think that we have a deal'.

The rules for agents for corporations are similar to those for companies.

CHAPTER 6

The Letter of Intent

> This chapter sets out the rules that apply to 'Letters of Intent/ Instructions to Proceed', and how they work. It then gives a graphic example of how they can go wrong if not used carefully.

In Step 8 of the example given in Chapter 5 the purchaser issued a 'Letter of Intent' to the contractor, who then commenced work. This is a convenient point to deal with the subject.

THE PRINCIPLES

A 'Letter of Intent' is a document sent by a potential purchaser to the potential contractor that creates a non-contractual obligation to pay for work done by the contractor in accordance with the terms set out in the document.

The term 'Letter of Intent (to award a contract)' is a jargon term. It has nothing to do with the Intent to make a contract referred to in Chapter 5. Nor is it simply a letter advising the contractor that the purchaser intends to award a contract to him. It is very much more than that. It is an 'instruction to proceed' with the work *before* the contract has been made.

It may be a letter, but it does not have to be. It could be in the form of a 'memorandum' or a 'notice' for instance. It could be in the form of a telex or a document sent through the post or hand-delivered. The form does not matter. What does matter is the content. It must be a written statement by the purchaser to the contractor stating that:

1. the purchaser intends to place a contract with the contractor, and

2. the purchaser wishes the contractor to commence the work, before signature of the contract, and

3. the purchaser requests, authorises or instructs the contractor to commence the work before the contract is agreed and signed.

If a Letter of Intent does not include points 2 and 3 above then it will not be a Letter of Intent, and should not be treated as such.

The practical problem for the contractor is often deciding whether a letter that looks like a Letter of Intent actually is one or not. The legal test is simply whether it is reasonable to assume that the purchaser is authorising him to commence work. Never confuse a statement of an 'intent to purchase' with an 'instruction to proceed'. The first without the second would not give him any authorisation. The second without the first could do so.

APPLICATION OF THE LAW

Under English (and Scottish) law a Letter of Intent is neither a contract nor is it part of contract law. It comes within a quite separate but related area of law – now called the Law of Restitution. Restitution covers a small number of situations where fairness requires the parties to behave almost as though a contract or something very similar to a contract existed between them. (Another such situation is where money is paid to the wrong person by mistake.) The old name for restitution law was 'quasi-contract' or 'rather like a contract'.

Every other system allows for Letters of Intent as well. (They are far too useful, not to be allowed.) However different legal systems treat them in different ways. Some treat them in the same way as the UK. Some treat them as separate contracts, which are replaced by the full contract. Others give them special status as a 'preliminary contract'. The result however is the same.

The rules are:

- A Letter of Intent can request but not require the contractor to carry out the work.

- The contractor is entitled to refuse to commence the work if he does not wish to do so.

- If the contractor does decide to carry out work, he must comply with any conditions set out in the Letter of Intent.

- But the contractor will then be entitled to be paid by the purchaser for the work that he does, provided that his work is of reasonable quality.

- If a contract then comes into force, the work done under the Letter of Intent will be paid for under the terms of the contract.

- If no contract comes into force the contractor will be entitled to be paid the reasonable costs (plus profit) of carrying out the work, provided that it is of reasonable quality.

- Both contractor and purchaser can terminate the arrangement at any time.

COMPLIANCE

The contractor does not have to comply with a Letter of Intent if he does not wish to do so. If the parties have made a contract the contractor does have an obligation to carry out the work. But the contractor is not obliged to accept the Letter of Intent or to carry out work under it.

PAYMENT UNDER A LETTER OF INTENT

Two bits of dog Latin in the same sentence is not a good idea. However the normal basis for payment for work done under a quasi-contract is on a *quantum meruit* basis. *Quantum meruit* simply means 'as much as it deserves', or 'what it is worth', in other words a reasonable amount for the actual quantity of work done. The basic theory is that where a contractor does work under contract then he is paid according to the terms laid down in the contract. Under a Letter of Intent no price applies. Therefore the contractor is to be paid a reasonable amount, which will be the cost of the work that he does, provided that the work has been done properly, plus a reasonable profit.

WHEN TO USE A LETTER OF INTENT

Agreeing all the terms of a complex contract can often take a long time, so that the purchaser cannot always wait for contract negotiations to be complete before the contractor commences work. In that case the purchaser may well decide to start the contractor working on the project while contract negotiations are still being finalised.

Once the contract is signed the Letter of Intent will come to an end. The work done by the contractor under the Letter will then become part of the contract and be paid for as a part of the contract.

HOW THE LETTER OF INTENT SHOULD BE USED

Clearly, once the contractor has been given a Letter of Intent, if he decides to accept it, he will expect to commence the work and to continue with that work for as long as the Letter of Intent is in place. He will also expect to be paid for the work that he will do. Therefore the purchaser should not place any Letter of Intent until he knows that:

- the project will go ahead;
- money is available to pay the contractor;
- the contractor knows what work is required; and
- contract negotiations are sufficiently well advanced for there to be no further major problems.

In addition the purchaser must understand that when he gives a contractor a Letter of Intent he is authorising that contractor to spend potentially a considerable amount of money. The purchaser therefore needs always to consider whether to include in the Letter of Intent any limitations upon the freedom of the contractor. Any limitations that are included in a Letter of Intent will be binding. Typical limitations might be that:

- the contractor should not incur expenditure above a certain figure without the further approval of the purchaser;

- the contractor should not work for more than a certain period without the further approval of the purchaser;

- work should be limited to design, or only that necessary to place sub-contracts or to reserve factory space and so on; and

- work should be done on the basis only of the specifications and conditions so far agreed between the parties.

The other thing that the purchaser must realise is that the Letter of Intent cannot impose liability on the contractor. It can lay down limits on what the purchaser must pay, but it cannot impose liability for being late, or for the consequences of poor work, for example. This can only be done by the contract itself. Therefore the purchaser will always need to replace the Letter of Intent with the contract fairly quickly.

CANCELLING A LETTER OF INTENT

It is rare for this to happen. However, either party can simply terminate the Letter of Intent by notice to the other. In that case the purchaser will be responsible for paying the contractor for all work done by the contractor up to the time of termination. This of course is very different to the position under a contract. Under a contract early termination of the work by either side, unless there is a specific clause in the contract permitting termination, would be a breach of contract.

THE BENEFITS OF A LETTER OF INTENT

For the purchaser the benefit of the Letter of Intent is that it gives him the opportunity to get work on his project started early, before the contract negotiations are complete. In addition he can also achieve an early finish date for the work. It is regularly the practice for a Letter of Intent to include a clause stating that the period for completion shall commence, not from the date of the contract, but from the date of the Letter of Intent.

From the point of view of the contractor the benefit is that he gets early and concrete evidence of the commitment of his purchaser. Starting work under a Letter of Intent does take some of the time pressure from the contractor as well. Finally of course the contractor must gain some increase in negotiating power once the letter is issued.

A CAUTIONARY TALE

This seems a very odd point to discuss. However, one of the very few cases that has actually come before the High Court relating to a Letter of Intent was also an excellent example of how *not* to use it.

The purchaser wished to buy parts for use in carrying out a major contract for the supply and installation of structural steelwork on site in the Middle East. The purchaser was in negotiation with the contractor for the supply of those parts. For various reasons the price offered by the contractor was very competitive, and negotiations were proceeding very well.

The purchaser therefore wrote to the contractor as follows:

> We are pleased to advise you that it is (our) intention to enter into a sub-contract with your company for the supply and delivery of the (equipment) on this project.
> The Price will be as quoted.
> The form of contract to be entered into will be our standard form of sub-contract … a copy of which is enclosed for your consideration.
> We enclose specifications.
> We request that you proceed immediately with the works pending at the preparation and issue to you of the official form of sub-contract.

There were no qualifications to this letter.

The contractor commenced work on the manufacture of the parts, and did his best. Then a number of things happened. First the contractor refused to accept the purchaser's 'standard form of sub-contract' as it stood, because it simply sought to impose on him total liability on a back-to-back basis to that of the purchaser under his own subcontract. Then it became obvious that the purchaser's delivery requirements were going to prove extremely difficult for the contractor to meet. Then the purchaser required fairly extensive design changes. Then the purchaser refused payment because items were delivered late, and the contractor withheld delivery because of non-payment. And so on.

The result was that for various reasons no subcontract was signed, and the contractor failed to meet the delivery requirements of the purchaser. As a result the purchaser was seriously late in completing his work.

The price originally agreed between the purchaser and contractor for the parts had been approximately £209 000. As a result of the purchaser's lateness his customer imposed lateness damages on him of £875 000. The purchaser thereupon sent to the contractor an invoice for £666 000, that is to say £875 000 less £209 000. The contractor flatly refused to pay, and instead claimed for payment for the equipment that he had supplied, and the whole affair ended up in court.

The judge decided that there was no contract. The only document between the parties of any significance was the letter. The judge decided that this was a Letter of Intent. Therefore the contractor was entitled to be paid a reasonable sum for the work that he had done. (The agreed contract price had been £209 000, remember.) The actual cost incurred by the contractor in the manufacture and supply of the parts was approximately £210 000. The judge therefore awarded the contractor the sum of £210 000 plus 10 per cent profit, that is a total of £231 000.

The judge dismissed the purchaser's claim for the enormous losses suffered as a result of the contractor's lateness. Effectively, said the judge, the only way the claim could have been valid would have been if a contract had been signed which entitled the purchaser to make that claim. No contract had been signed; therefore the only right that existed was the right of the contractor to receive payment of a reasonable sum for the work they had done. And so the purchaser suffered a very painful, and costly, lesson.

What mistakes had the purchaser made? Of course it is always easy to be wise after the event. But perhaps:

- not leaving himself enough time for a complex contract negotiation, and therefore,

- placing a Letter of Intent too early, while there were still serious issues to negotiate, and therefore,

- suffering a major loss of bargaining power in those negotiations, and

- not completing the contract negotiation and placing the contract,

- so that he was left with no grounds to claim anything back from the contractor, presumably because of a

- failure to understand the difference between a contract and a Letter of Intent.

CHAPTER 7

The Meanings Behind the Words

This chapter looks at the problems of contract interpretation – how the lawyer works out what the words that have been used in the contract actually do mean – if and when there is a dispute. We all need to be able to second-guess the lawyers.

THE PROBLEM OF WORDS

This is the most difficult area for most people. It is difficult for three reasons:

- When we start talking words in contracts we find ourselves dealing, not just with law, but with lawyers. Lawyers are very good at words. Just as accountants are very good at sums, lawyers are good at writing things down. Because they are good at words, they can scare people.

- It is all too easy to get the words wrong. As Winston Churchill once said 'words are tricky little b———s'. English is a very flexible language, with lots of words that have two or more different meanings.

- We are not very good at quality control when we deal with words.

THE BASIC PRINCIPLE

The commercial contract in writing is presumed to be a 'complete' and 'precise' statement of the terms agreed between the parties. This means two things. If it isn't included in the written document (or referred to, 'included by reference', in the written document), it is not part of the contract. If it is in the written document, it is part of the contract.

The law then sees its job as providing a remedy for any party if the other party has failed to carry out its contract obligations properly.

HOW THE LAW SEES THE COMMERCIAL ORGANISATION

We have already said that the company is automatically expected to know what it is doing when it enters into a contract. Even more important, the law also presumes that the company knows what it is saying when it enters into a contract. The law automatically assumes that the company has agreed to the precise words that are written into the contract and is prepared to take the risks and liabilities that go with those words.

Therefore once a contract is made, the company must live with the words, whatever they may be, for the duration. Of course you may agree to change the words, or to have 'agreed interpretations' of some of the words. And in real life nobody is bothered by the thousands of minor mistakes in carrying out contracts that happen every day. Nevertheless the principle holds good. The law expects the company to have the necessary language skills to say what it intends, and therefore presumes that the commercial contract means what it says, when interpreted correctly, that is by a lawyer.

This is pretty well a universal principle, applicable to all commercial contracts everywhere. Common law and civil law are identical.

A REASONABLE PERSON

The words used in a contract mean what a 'reasonable' (and impartial) person, knowing the factual background to the contract, would think that they meant.

A reasonable person is one with the appropriate skills and knowledge to understand the contract. A contract made between two engineering companies will mean what a reasonable person with word skills and engineering knowledge would think that the words mean when he reads the contract. A contract between two insurance companies will mean what a reasonable person with knowledge of the insurance industry would think that they meant when he reads the contract – and so on.

WHO IS A REASONABLE PERSON?

The problem is that if your company is involved in a contract, you are not the reasonable person. Even though you know what the words are supposed to mean, you are not 'impartial' in legal terms. This is because you are employed by one of the parties to that contract. The people employed by the other company involved are in the same position. An impartial person has to be an outsider.

The choice is limited. You may ask an expert in the industry, or a mediator or conciliator, but if there is no other way of resolving the dispute you may have no choice but to ask a judge, arbitrator or adjudicator. The problem is that the judge is not a reasonable industry expert with good technical word skills. He is a lawyer and lawyers are seldom expert in industry or technology. But they do have incredible legal word skills; they spend their entire working lives using words. And although an arbitrator or adjudicator may understand your world, he has an obligation to make his decision in 'a judicial manner', that is very broadly in the same way as a judge.

The way a judge will reach his decision is that he will listen to the arguments of the advocates, in the UK probably barristers, who present the case for both sides. He will then make his decision only on the basis of the legal arguments that they have put to him. An arbitrator or adjudicator has to take a similar approach.

Therefore if one of your contracts becomes the subject of a dispute, the words that you have written into the contract will be subject to the interpretation of professional lawyers. Lawyers might not interpret the words of the contract in the way that people in the industry would interpret them. They will interpret words in the way that lawyers interpret words and, in an imperfect world, you have to live with this.

THINGS TO LOOK OUT FOR

1. The terms of the contract can be of different kinds – conditions, warranties and innominate, or intermediate, terms. The law here is rather confusing.

2. Words and grammar – it is all too easy to say something different to what we wanted to say.

3. Organising the contract properly – to avoid unnecessary mistakes.

THE ROLE OF TERMS

CONDITION

The word 'condition' can be used in contracts in two ways. Firstly it can mean one of the terms of the contract, as opposed, for example, to the specification. Secondly, in lawyers' jargon, it can mean a particular type of contract term. This second meaning is what concerns us here.

The condition is a major promise, a significant term of the contract. If the party that has made that promise fails to carry it out, the other party is entitled either to claim damages for the failure to comply, or to terminate the contract and claim the damages as well. The damages claimable will be all of the losses that the injured party can prove that he has suffered as a direct result of the breach (see Chapter 8).

WARRANTY

The warranty (also lawyers' jargon) is a less important promise, a minor term of the contract. If the party that has made that promise fails to carry it out, the injured party is entitled to claim damages for the losses that he has suffered as a result, but will not be allowed to terminate the contract. He must live with the contract as performed.

INNOMINATE OR INTERMEDIATE TERM

An Innominate or Intermediate Term is neither a condition nor a warranty, but has elements of both. In such a case a serious breach of the term would entitle the injured party to terminate and/or claim damages, whereas a minor breach would permit only a claim for damages.

TERMS IN PRACTICE

As you can see already the only practical differences between the three types of term is in the rights the injured party will have against the other if there is breach of contract. All three give the injured party the right to claim damages. The problem is when a contract can be terminated.

Of course the usual commercial solution is to avoid argument by simply including a 'termination clause' in the contract conditions, allowing for termination of the contract in the case of any breach of the terms of the contract which is not remedied by the party at fault within a reasonable period.

HOW DID WE GET TO WHERE WE ARE NOW?

Traditionally English law recognised only conditions and warranties. This meant that whenever there was a dispute about whether a contract had been properly terminated for breach or not the judge always had to decide whether a contract clause was a condition or a warranty.

There was, and is, no hard and fast rule. Whether any particular term of the contract is a condition or a warranty will depend upon the words used in the contract. Some promises are almost automatically conditions, such as delivery date or that the goods should comply with the specification. Then the contract may make a particular clause a condition – 'it is a condition of this contract that ...' – and so on.

Although this applied to the majority of cases there are one or two cases in which judges held that terms of the contract stated to be conditions were not really conditions but merely warranties, with no right of termination for breach. All of these cases however concerned slightly unusual contracts. In the standard purchase/procurement situation it is reasonably safe to say that if a clause in the contract is stated to be a condition then it will be.

THE INNOMINATE TERM

There was a series of cases during the 1950s and '60s involving contracts for the purchase of second-hand cars. The typical situation was that a purchaser had bought a second-hand car and then was dissatisfied with the car because of defects in it. He had tried to return the car to the dealer and ask for his money back. The dealer would refuse to take the car back but would offer the purchaser a small amount of money off the contract price or would undertake to try and repair the defects.

The dispute would always turn on the proper interpretation of the terms of the contract under which the car was bought and in particular of the way that the dealer had described the car (that is the specification). The description of the car would be that the car was 'in perfect condition' or was 'very reliable', or something of that nature. There would be no doubt that the car was defective, and there would be no doubt that the defects in the car were in breach of the wording of the contract. The nub of the dispute would be whether or not the purchaser had the right to return the car to the dealer. If the term of the contract was a condition then the purchaser would have the right to terminate the contract (and return the car and get his money back). If the term in the contract was merely a warranty then the purchaser would not have the right to return the car to the dealer but would have to accept repair work or money off the price.

The cases led to a series of judgements in which judges produced convoluted arguments as to whether or not particular words in a particular contract were to be interpreted as a condition or a warranty. Of course what the judges really were doing was looking at the state of the car and asking themselves whether the purchaser should have the right to walk away from the contract. If they decided that the purchaser should have the right to walk away they would call the words a condition. If they felt that he should not have the right to walk away they would call the words a warranty. Not surprisingly, this led to a number of dubious decisions, and finally the courts did accept that 'reverse reasoning' was taking place.

The solution to this problem was created in a case involving Kawasaki Motorcycles – *Kawasaki KKK v Hong Kong Fir Shipping Ltd*. In this case the court held that it was possible for a term of the contract to be neither a condition nor a warranty, but somewhere between the two, what the court called an 'Innominate' or 'Intermediate Term'. In such a case a serious breach of the term would entitle the injured party to terminate and/or claim damages, whereas a minor breach would permit only a claim for damages. In theory this is a perfect solution to the problem of the rights of the injured party in any case of breach of the contract.

However, the Kawasaki dispute arose because Kawasaki had a contract to hire a ship to transport motorcycles from Japan to other countries. The contract, a charter party, was for a period of 21 months. In the contract there were clauses that the ship was to be in good condition, and the crew efficient. A series of problems caused by bad seamanship and seriously defective steering gear and engines kept the ship out of action for almost all the first three months of the contract. Kawasaki terminated the contract. But when the case got to court, four years later, the court decided that the clauses were innominate terms and that the breach had not been serious enough to entitle Kawasaki to terminate. The result was that although the shipping company was in breach of contract and wholly at fault, it won heavy damages for wrongful termination from Kawasaki who was not in any way to blame.

The problem is obvious: because the innominate term does not create a clear-cut situation, it can simply create a lottery as to what the courts may decide in any instance several years after the event if one party terminates and the other disputes that decision. It is therefore perhaps best avoided by making the important terms clearly stated conditions and leaving everything else as a warranty – and then including a termination clause anyway.

CIVIL LAW

Civil law takes a radically different approach to common law. Common law says that the terms of the contract can be of different types, so that breach of different types of term will have different consequences. Civil law takes the opposite view. Under civil law all terms of the contract are equal in status. Their status is similar to that of a warranty under English law. Therefore the only basic right that either party has for breach of any term of a contract is to claim damages for the results of the breach. Damages will be assessed on, effectively, the same basis as under common law.

Therefore neither party to the contract has the power to terminate the contract for breach, unless there is a specific termination clause in the contract. If there is no such clause in the contract the only way to terminate the contract is by going to court and asking for a court order to terminate the contract, (effectively suing the other party for breach – which takes time and costs money). As a result it is normal practice for all commercial contracts in civil law countries to include a termination clause.

INTERPRETATION

The aim is to derive from the contract 'a common sense interpretation so as to give effect to the commercial purpose of the parties to the contract'. The difficulty is that once the parties are in dispute this may not always be possible.

A FOUR-STAGE PROCESS

1. Ascertain all the background knowledge reasonably available to both (or all) the parties at the time of the contract. This background includes

anything that would affect the way in which the contract should be understood. However it excludes previous negotiations between the parties and any statements they have made which have not become part of the contract. This has been called the 'factual matrix'.

2.   Decide what the words of the contract mean.The words of the contract must be given their 'natural and ordinary meaning'. In other words the basic principle is that the parties are deemed to have intended to use the words they did actually use.

3.   Decide what the parties would reasonably have understood the words of the contract to mean against the relevant background.

4.   Apply this interpretation to the actual dispute that has arisen.

Remember that contracts can be very different. Some contracts contain very little information, and the only way to give them a commonsense interpretation is to look at the background. For instance a contract with a bank for an overdraft says nothing about why the borrower wanted the money or why the bank manager decided it was a good risk. Then it is essential to look at the background. However in the complex contract normal within engineering and technology most of the factual matrix is in fact already in the contract. Our contracts contain masses of factual information about what equipment and services are to be supplied, how they are to be supplied, what they are to be used for, details of the site, and so on. The more information there is in the contract the more important Stage 2 above becomes, and the less important Stages 1 and 3.

HOW DOES THE LAW INTERPRET A CONTRACT?

It does this by a process of careful interpretation of the exact words used in the contract (Stage 2 above), in order to determine *precisely* what the bargain is that the parties have actually made. It is therefore essential to be extremely careful how words are used when writing contracts.

This is going to be a very long answer to a simple question, but a lot of explanation is necessary.

(In theory civil law pays less attention to precise interpretation than common law, preferring to emphasise the need for the parties to carry out their commercial obligations in a proper manner. In practice the civil law approach to the wording of a complex contract is very similar to a strict interpretation – the common law approach.)

The problem is language, especially the English language
English is the most flexible language in the modern world. However with a contract the flexibility of English can become a problem. It is possible for the words used in a

contract to have a wide range of different meanings unless great care has been taken over how we do it.

Flexibility of language can create ambiguity: 'PERFECT POLISH' can mean four different things depending on how we pronounce it. Consider a notice in a local newspaper in spring. 'Put your clocks forward one hour before you go to bed on Saturday night'. Now compare that with 'Before you go to bed on Saturday night put your clocks forward one hour'. The second statement has one meaning but the first has two. Changing the order of the words can create or eliminate a problem. The reason for the ambiguity in this example is that the phrase 'one hour' can either be attached to 'put your clocks forward' (by how much) or 'before you go to bed' (when). Of course, one of these interpretations looks perverse as we all know what the newspaper meant to say. That is *precisely* the problem. Because we know what we mean to say, we can sometimes fail to see exactly what we have said.

Grammar is always a potential problem. Most of us, if we take care over our sentences, are reasonably competent in the language and can get the grammar correct. If, however, we get the grammar wrong then the words used may have a different meaning to the one that we intended.

In a high court case ten years ago the judge had to consider a contract provision: 'The Contractor shall do xxxxx and yyyyy in accordance with a specification.' The learned judge decided that this meant that the contractor was required to carry out yyyyy in accordance with the specification. He also had to carry out xxxxx, but xxxxx did not have to comply with the specification. However, said the judge, if the contract had said 'The Contractor shall do *both* xxxxx *and* yyyyy in accordance with the specification….', then his decision would have been different.

This decision might look totally perverse, but all that the judge has done is to read the words and then ask himself what those words in that grammatical framework actually meant. Of course the reason for the dispute was that the contractor had failed to comply with the specification and was looking for an excuse for not having done so; however in one sense the judge had little choice. The purchaser had written the words, and got the grammar wrong; so the purchaser had to stand the consequences. Where any party writes their own words into the contract they have to take the risk of getting the words wrong. A judge will always tend to interpret their mistakes in the other side's favour (what is called the 'contra proferentem' rule).

There can also problems associated with the meanings of words. A word like 'hepatitis' has one meaning as it is a very specific technical term relating to a well-defined type of medical condition. However some words have several different meanings. 'Tack' for instance has 14. When a word that has several different meanings is used in a contract, it might mean any one of those different things. The problem is therefore to manipulate the language of the contract to eliminate the unwanted meanings.

As an example consider the noun 'bit'. 'Bit' is related to the verb 'to bite'. It therefore means two basic things: first something that may bite into something else, and secondly things that might have been bitten off something else. In other words it has two basic categories of meaning: the first 'things that cut into other things or act upon other things', and secondly 'small amounts of things or bite-sized pieces'.

Then the word has different kinds of meaning. First it has a series of meanings that can be classified as ordinary, everyday meanings. These meanings will be such as 'piece', 'part', 'small coin' and so on. Then the word has jargon meanings. Jargon is immensely valuable in any area of technology or skill. It is the specialised use of words, giving those words very specific meanings within the context of the particular technology or skill in which they are being used. Every discipline uses jargon. Lawyers and accountants use jargon. Different professional engineering disciplines have different jargon. As a jargon word the word 'bit' means one thing to a drilling engineer, something totally different to a computer programmer, and something different again to a jockey or a locksmith.

Finally the word also has a series of colloquial meanings, centred round the idea of 'a small amount'. These meanings appear in such phrases as 'I'll be there in a bit', 'a bit of a laugh', 'a bit of a do' or 'a bit of a problem'.

In a dispute the judge can decide, if he feels that it is appropriate to do so on the basis of the evidence and legal argument, to give the words whatever meaning he thinks that those words ought to have, even if one or both of the parties disagree.

Get a good dictionary

The basic rule is that words in the contract will normally have their ordinary, everyday, meaning. If the contract, or the commercial context of the contract, makes it clear that words are to have a jargon meaning, then the words will be given a jargon meaning. They might also be given a colloquial meaning but that is very rare in commercial contracts.

The rule of interpretation of words in accordance with their ordinary everyday meaning is that the words will be given the precise meaning stated in an authoritative dictionary. Where a jargon meaning is to be applied then again it is the precise definition given in the dictionary that will apply. Only when a colloquial meaning is to be applied will the courts take into account what the parties actually *thought* the words should mean. In simple terms, the words in commercial contracts do not mean what the draftsman thinks or hopes they mean: they mean what the dictionary says they mean. It is essential for anyone working with contracts to have a comprehensive dictionary.

THE PRINCIPLES IN PRACTICE

THE JUDGE'S DECISION

Often when a judge decides a case he will say something like 'Applying the well-known principle of interpretation that ... it is clear that the contract means ...' There are literally dozens of principles of interpretation applied by the courts when they interpret documents, and it is impossible to state or discuss them all here. Some apply particularly to special kinds of documents such as leases or legislation. Many however apply to contracts.

Principles of interpretation are important because they demonstrate how the judge/lawyer approaches a contract. The judge will pick whichever principle suits his purpose, and use it to justify his decision.

You will see that there is a common theme running through them, that the commercial company must live by the words that it uses. Therefore it is vitally important for the commercial company to get the words correct. In practice far too many disputes turn upon the interpretation of 'incorrect' words used in the contract. Some of the more important principles are given here.

- 'The construction of a contract is a matter of law. The meaning of words is a matter of fact.' In other words the judge has the right to impose his meaning on the contract words, using the factual meaning/definitions of those words in grammatical and dictionary terms.

- 'For the purpose of the construction of a contract the parties mean the words they have used.' If you say something that is different to what you intended to say you will have to live with the consequences, unless of course both parties are agreed that the words should be changed.

- 'The words of the contract shall have their precise but ordinary everyday meaning.' 'Bit' means a piece part or small quantity.

- 'The words of the contract must be read in a way that ensures the technical effectiveness of the contract.' 'Bit' means a drill bit and so on.

- 'The words must be interpreted in the way they were understood by the parties at the time they made the contract.' Colloquial meanings can apply.

- 'The intentions of the parties must be ascertained from the language they have used, considered in the light of the surrounding circumstances and the object of the contract, so far as that has been agreed or proved.' You have to live with what the contract actually says, not what you wanted to say, but failed or forgot to say.

- 'The court will generally adopt an objective approach. It will consider what would have been the intention of reasonable persons in the position of the parties to the contract.' This is because that is what the other party has a right to expect.

- 'Where the words of a contract have a clear meaning that meaning must apply.'

- 'Preliminary contract drafts and preparatory negotiations may not in general be used to interpret a contract. But a previous agreement may be relied upon to interpret a later contract made pursuant to it.' Because we may change our minds during negotiations.

- 'Where a contract is made wholly in writing no other terms can apply.'

- In any case where a contract is based upon a model form of contract the court is reluctant to disturb the established interpretation.' But the judge may interpret modifications to the model terms against the party that wrote them into the contract.

- 'The words of the contract should be construed in their grammatical and ordinary sense except to the extent that some modification is necessary to avoid inconsistency or absurdity.'

- 'Words will always be given the meaning that they had at the time that the contract was signed. If meanings change later on that will not affect the meaning of the contract.'

- 'It is permissible (and almost normal practice) to be prepared to imply terms into a consumer contract. The presumption however is against implying terms into written contracts. The more complete and detailed the written contract the harder it is to imply a term into that contract. If a term is to be implied into a commercial contract, it has to be one that is so obvious that neither party would have objected at the time.' Very few terms can be taken as read in commercial contracts.

Then two principles of major importance:

- 'The only term that is always implied into a written commercial contract is that neither party shall prevent the other party from performing its side of the contract and that where performance of the contract cannot take place without the cooperation of both parties, then cooperation shall be forthcoming.' Preventing the other side from carrying out its work is breach of contract.

- 'Where a contract does not expressly or by necessary implication fix a time for the performance of any contractual obligation the law implies that it shall be performed within a reasonable time.'

THE CANONS OF CONSTRUCTION

These are the golden rules that judges apply when digging the correct meaning out of complex documents. They are no different to any other principles of interpretation:

- 'In order to arrive at the true interpretation of any document a clause must not be considered in isolation but must be considered in the context of the whole of the document. In construing a contract all parts of it must be given effect where possible, and no part of it should be treated as inoperative or surplus.' Don't try to take words out of context.

- 'Where the contract is a standard form of contract to which the parties have added special conditions, greater weight must be given to the special conditions, and in case of conflict between the general conditions and the special conditions, the latter will prevail.'

- 'When the contract expressly mentions some things, it is often to be inferred that other things of the same general category which are not expressly mentioned were deliberately omitted.' This rule is sometimes given a Latin tag *expressio unius exclusio alterius* – saying one thing excludes the others.

- 'If a contract lists a number of things of the same general category, but then does allow other things to be included (for example, in a *force majeure* clause), then other things can only be considered to be included if they are of the same kind as those things already listed.' Another Latin tag *eiusdem generis*.

- 'A contract will be construed so far as possible in such a manner as not to permit one party to it to take advantage of his own wrong.'

- 'A statement in a document will be ambiguous when it has two or more meanings each of which can apply without distorting the words. If the ambiguity is latent (in other words a hidden problem only shows up when you try to carry out the contract), then external evidence can be taken to try to resolve the ambiguity. If the ambiguity cannot be resolved the contract or clause is invalid.' Because it is uncertain.

- 'Patent ambiguity exists when a document has two or more meanings right from the start. Where there is patent ambiguity in a document which forms part of a contract the court can refer to subsidiary, that is, lower-ranking, documents in the contract, if they will resolve the ambiguity.' 'Put your clocks forward one hour before you go to bed' is an example of patent ambiguity.

- 'A contract, or a clause in a contract, is uncertain if it is impossible to decide what it really means. If a clause or a contract is uncertain then that clause or contract is invalid.'

CHAPTER 8

Lateness, Specifications and Defects

Most contracts are carried out successfully. Unfortunately some are not. The areas where contracts get into difficulties are often fairly predictable. This chapter therefore deals with the law relating to three of the most difficult areas in contracts – areas where argument and dispute are always likely.

LIABILITY FOR LATENESS

THE LAW'S APPROACH

In the commercial contract all obligations must be completed by the time stated. If no time is stated in the contract then the obligation must be completed within a reasonable time. The contractor always has more to do – therefore basic law always favours the purchaser in principle – but remember that the purchaser usually has time obligations as well.

There is very little difference between English law and civil law systems, except in relation to the law on *force majeure* clauses (see below).

THE RISK

Lateness is a serious risk for both parties.

It is a risk for the contractor because:

- Every contractor is late part of the time. Most delays are only small, but some delays will always be more substantial.

- It is impossible for the contractor to predict at the date of contract:
  - how late he will be;
  - why he will be late – his own fault, delay by the purchaser or something outside his control; and

– what effect any late delivery will really have upon the purchaser (this is dependent on factors of which the contractor has no control or knowledge).

It is a risk for the purchaser because:

- He also cannot predict what lateness might occur and why and how it will affect him.

- Going to law to claim redress is not much use most of the time. The cost is high, and he can only claim damages in court when he is able to *prove* the losses he has actually suffered. In practice this is often harder than it may seem; knowledge is not proof.

THE LAW ON LATENESS

There are three, and only three, possible contractual situations allowed by the UK law of contract in regard to the delivery dates in a contract:

- time 'of the essence'

- estimated delivery date

- liquidated damages for late delivery.

TIME IS 'OF THE ESSENCE'

The law has always been that the time promise, for delivery of equipment or completion of work, is a major term of the commercial contract. Therefore any promise to deliver or complete by a fixed date or within a fixed period is to be regarded as a contract *condition*, or in the words of a Victorian judge 'of the essence' of the contract.

It is not necessary for the contract actually to state that time is of the essence of the contract, although many sets of conditions of purchase will contain phrases such as 'time is of the essence', or 'delivery dates are of fundamental importance'. The mere fact that a fixed date or period is stated for delivery/completion is enough.

THE RULE IN OPERATION

If a contractor takes a contract to carry out work, or supply equipment or complete the erection/commissioning of equipment on site by a stated date or within a fixed period, in the absence of any qualification of that statement, the date or period will be a contract condition. Therefore if the contractor is late, even if only by (in one case) fifteen minutes, the purchaser may, if he wishes:

- claim damages for breach of contract (see below), and

- treat the contract as cancelled and reject the equipment.

In building contracts where a fixed date for completion is stated, time is not of the essence. However this simply means that the purchaser cannot cancel the contract if the contractor is late. There is nothing to prevent the purchaser claiming damages.

ESTIMATED DELIVERY DATE

Whenever there is no delivery/completion date stated in the contract, the law is that the contractor's obligations must still be completed within a reasonable time. Where a contract sets a date for delivery or completion but then states that the date is either approximate or an estimate, then the contractor has to carry out his obligations within a reasonable time of that date.

THE RULE IN OPERATION

If the contractor fails to deliver or complete within a reasonable time, then the purchaser can claim against him just as if he had failed to meet a fixed date in a time of the essence situation.

There is no specific definition of what constitutes a reasonable time. In practice, all other things being equal, this will normally depend on the length of the delivery/ completion period. Anything up to 10 per cent over the original period might be deemed to be reasonable.

Are these rules adequate?

They are adequate for minor contracts, perhaps, but not for large contracts. In large contracts they present problems for both purchaser and contractor. For the contractor the problems are obvious. There is no right to an extension of the delivery or completion period if he is delayed for reasons that are beyond his control. If he is late he is in a difficult situation in that he knows that he may very well be liable for damages, but he will have no way of knowing how large those damages may be.

Whatever benefit going to law to claim damages gives the purchaser, it totally fails to ensure that he gets his contract completed quickly. In most cases what the purchaser really needs is to achieve the earliest completion even if it is a little late. What he does not want to do is to risk losing his contract completely and then to have to go through the whole business all over again with another contractor. Therefore what the purchaser needs is a device that will push the contractor towards minimising lateness rather than something that can be used only to attack a contractor after lateness has occurred. It is these problems which lead most purchasers and contractors to modify the basic solutions given above.

LIQUIDATED DAMAGES AND *FORCE MAJEURE* CLAUSES

The contract will state a fixed delivery/completion date plus a liquidated damages clause and a *force majeure* clause. The liquidated damages clause will push the contractor towards minimising lateness in delivery and help the purchaser to claim damages without actually having to prove too much in the way of losses. The *force majeure* clause then deals with the contractor's concerns about delays that are not his fault. There are a few principles of law to be explained here, but the explanations are necessary to understand how the law works.

Liquidated damages law

- 'Liquidated' is simply lawyers jargon for 'pre-agreed' (damages).

- The theory of liquidated damages is that where, at the date of contract, the parties are aware that a breach of contract might occur, (such as being late), but they do not know at that time what the actual consequences of the breach might be, they can agree a 'reasonable pre-estimate' of the loss which might be caused by the breach and write that pre-estimate into the contract. Then, if the breach does happen, the estimated amount will be payable instead of the actual losses suffered.

- Reasonable pre-estimates of loss can vary widely, depending on how optimistic or pessimistic we are. So *any* figures that can be shown to be possible will be acceptable.

- Therefore the pre-estimate need not be true or accurate as long as it is possible and agreed by the parties.

Liquidated damages clauses are a very good example of the bargain element in contracts. Once the parties have agreed their liquidated damages the law will not ask whether the bargain is a fair one or not, provided that it is within the rules – it will simply enforce it.

However there is one essential element of a liquidated damages clause. If the reasonable pre-estimate definition is a little thin, it is important that the clause should not be a penalty clause instead of a damages clause. A penalty is something that is there with the aim, in the eyes of the law, of punishing the party in breach rather than compensating the party injured by the breach. (A penalty clause might be 'Liability for any late delivery shall be £250 000'.) It is not always easy to determine whether or not a clause is a damages clause or a penalty clause; the practical way of distinguishing between the two is to ask whether:

- the amount that would be charged by the clause changes according to the extent of the breach, and

- that amount could approximate to the losses that might, in one set of circumstances, actually be suffered by the purchaser.

If both answers are in the affirmative the clause is a damages clause and allowable. If not, the clause is penal and legally invalid. Then the purchaser cannot claim the contractual damages but he may still claim unliquidated damages on a 'time of essence' basis. In other words both parties are back at square one.

Force majeure *clause law*

Under English law there is no right to any extension of time (for either party) unless there is a clause in the contract that permits it. The clause must set out the reasons that justify the extension and the length of extension allowed. Such clauses are usually referred to as *force majeure* clauses. Most contracts will include a clause allowing an extension of the contract time if the contractor is delayed for reasons outside his normal control.

(Civil law is different. In most civil law countries the law automatically allows an extension of time if either party is delayed by 'act of god' or government action, such as war or trade embargo, even without a *force majeure* clause in the contract. However there are many other more likely causes of delay, so that usual practice is to include a full clause.)

There are two basic ways of writing a force majeure clause. One is to use a simple, but all-embracing, formula such as 'industrial dispute, delays due to the purchaser, or any cause beyond the reasonable control of one (or either) party'. The other is to list a whole series of possible causes of delay and then to add a phrase such as 'and other causes of delay', or to say that justifiable delays will 'include but not be limited to' the causes listed. There is a particular risk in this second method due to the *sui generis* interpretation rule (see Chapter 7). Where a clause lists several examples any further allowable instances must be similar to the items listed.

WHAT HAPPENS AT THE END OF THE LIQUIDATED DAMAGES PERIOD?

If the full liquidated damages payable under the contract have been paid and the work is still not complete, what happens then? There has not been a single decided case in the courts as to what the exact position is in these circumstances. There are three possibilities:

1. As soon as the limit set by the liquidated damages clause has been reached time is again of the essence of the contract and the ordinary law will apply.

2. The purchaser may give reasonable notice that he requires time to become of the essence of the contract. (One problem, of course, would be what

would constitutes 'reasonable' notice? If the contractor has been very much in delay, must the notice be long enough to give him a reasonable chance to complete?).

3. The purchaser has no further remedy until he can show that the contractor is in substantial breach of contract – that is to say when the contractor, by continuing failure to complete, has totally deprived the purchaser of almost all benefit that he might have obtained under the contract.

This third possibility is almost certainly the correct one. Once the full liquidated damages have been paid (especially when the liquidated damages clause contains a statement that the payment of liquidated damages is 'in full satisfaction of the contractor's liability for delay'), the purchaser cannot claim any further damages for late delivery until he can show substantial breach of contract by the contractor, unless there is a specific statement in the contract of the further rights that the purchaser has.

THE PURCHASER'S OBLIGATION

The rule for the purchaser is just the same as for the contractor. All his obligations have to be completed by the time stated in the contract, or within a reasonable time. If he fails to do so, he is in breach. Lateness by the purchaser is not normally treated as breach of a condition however but breach of a warranty. Therefore the contractor is not entitled to terminate the contract, but is entitled to damages – all the costs resulting from the delay caused by the purchaser's breach, and an extension to the contract period.

TIME AT LARGE

'Time at large' is a phrase used to describe a situation that can occasionally arise if a contract has been badly written. This situation is rare, but not entirely unknown. The basic legal rule is that the contractor must complete his obligations by the time stated in the contract. If, however, the purchaser does something that prevents the contractor completing his obligations on time, and there is no *force majeure* clause in the contract that allows an extension to the contract time-scale – in other words the purchaser has forced the contractor to complete late – then the contractor's time obligation is cancelled. The contractor must still complete, but can take as long as he needs to do so, with no liability. This is one reason why contracts usually need to contain adequate clauses dealing with delays caused by the purchaser or by variations.

THE SPECIFICATION

THE LAW'S APPROACH

There are basic rules that the contractor must have the right to sell the goods and give the purchaser the right to uncontested ownership. If a sale is by sample the goods must correspond to the sample. If sale is by weight, the goods must be weighed and so on. Then the equipment supplied or installed must comply with the 'description' given in the contract, (except in minor details). Work and services must also comply with the description given in the contract.

These requirements are implied conditions and cannot be excluded. (Theoretically – see Section 6(2)(a) of the Unfair Contract Terms Act – it is possible to exclude or limit liability, but in reality this could not happen except in perhaps a 'state-of-the-art' development contract, see below.) If the contractor does not comply, he is in breach and is liable for damages; the purchaser may also if he wishes terminate the contract.

Small failures to comply may be treated not as a breach of a condition, but as a breach of a warranty, or even as a breach of an innominate term, so that the purchaser might only be allowed to claim damages (see below).

THE IMPORTANCE OF THE SPECIFICATION

The specification is usually the most important part of the contract. It is also the longest and most complex document in the contract. Most of the conditions of contract, for instance, are there to provide administrative rules, or as contingency planning in case things go wrong. The specification is what the contractor always must do. It is the one part of the contract that is always crucial to success or failure. It is also the part of the contract that is hardest to write correctly for the purchaser, and understand correctly for the contractor. Specifications are regularly badly written by purchasers and/or misinterpreted by contractors. The law is easy to state; complying with it can be very difficult.

THE PRINCIPLES

There is no better way to explain the principles than to start by quoting the language of the relevant legislation.

Equipment and goods sold/supplied – Sale of Goods Act 1979 Section 13 (1–2): 'Where there is a contract for the sale of goods by description there is an implied [condition] that the goods will comply with the description.'

Equipment and goods installed – Supply of Goods and Services Act 1982 Section 1 (1–2): 'In this Act a "contract for the transfer of goods" means a contract under which one person transfers or agrees to transfer to another the property (ie ownership) in goods, other than … a contract of sale …'

Section 3 (1–2): 'Where, under a contract for the transfer of goods the transferor transfers or agrees to transfer the property in the goods by description … there is an implied condition that the goods will correspond with the description.'

The law is easy to explain when it applies to serious failures to comply with a specification – serious failure will be breach of a contract condition. The problem is to explain the law in relation to minor failures.

As a preliminary point, do remember that 'description' is not the same thing as 'specification'. Often the contract specification will contain a lot more than just the description of the equipment to be supplied or work to be done. Often too the description of the equipment or work will appear in other parts of the contract as well as in the specification.

We have already said that a significant breach of a description entitles the purchaser to claim damages or to terminate as well as claiming damages. If we go back 70 or 80 years we would see cases in which judges held that even minute breaches of description would entitle the purchaser to terminate the contract. However this is not the case today. If a judge decided that a particular part of the description was not a condition but an innominate term, as was the case in the Kawasaki case mentioned in Chapter 7 then the judge might not allow termination. Also it is established law that a minor breach of specification is not breach of a condition, but merely a breach of a warranty, and therefore, although the purchaser could claim damages, he would not be entitled to terminate the contract. (Of course there may always be argument about whether a breach is minor or not.)

In other words always look at the whole of the contract to decide what the description of the equipment or work actually it is, don't just look at the specification. Then remember that if there is a major breach of that description the purchaser can terminate; if there is a minor breach of that description the purchaser cannot terminate; but of course the purchaser can always claim damages.

Finally remember that a specification may well include quite a lot of terms of the contract that are not part of the description of the equipment or work. For instance inspection provisions may well be separate terms of the contract, independent of the description of the equipment. All these terms have to be treated as separate contract provisions.

LIABILITY FOR DEFECTIVE WORK AND EQUIPMENT

THE LAW'S APPROACH

There is a lot of law about the liability of a seller for defects in the goods that he has supplied. Most of this law is consumer protection law. Some applies to commercial contracts as well. The overall result is complex in detail, but easy to summarise:

- Equipment supplied or installed must be of satisfactory quality, fit for use for normal purposes, and (usually) also fit for the particular use intended by the purchaser, free of defects when supplied/installed, and defect-free for a reasonable period thereafter.

- These requirements are implied conditions of the contract. They apply in all contracts, unless excluded, or liability is limited by a term of the contract.

- In addition the contractor can also be liable for defective equipment or faulty work under the general law of negligence (see Chapter 11). Again liability under the law of negligence, as between contractor and purchaser, can also be excluded or limited by a term of the contract.

- Terms excluding or limiting liability under contract or in negligence will only be valid to the extent that they are reasonable.

RISK

Consequential damage claims arising out of the supply of defective equipment or negligent work on site are a major risk in equipment contracts. The reasons for this are:

- Human error makes it inevitable that defective equipment will be supplied from time to time and that accidents will take place on site.

- While in most cases defects in equipment or accidents will merely cause a brief machine breakdown or only minor damage, there is always the risk of a major claim because:
  - defective equipment or site negligence could cause a major disaster, causing damage of horrendous proportions, or
  - even minor damage can cause substantial losses if it has the effect of stopping a factory or plant from producing for a significant period.

The risk is always a problem for the contractor because:

- The basic principles of law are again totally on the purchaser's side – therefore, the contractor can only protect himself against enormous unlimited claims by taking positive steps to include protective clauses in his contracts.

- It is impossible to predict when and where there may be an accident or how serious the consequences of that accident might be. All one can say is that there is the possibility of a serious accident in every contract one handles.

THE LEGAL PRINCIPLES

There are three principal different types of liability in law under which the contractor can be held liable to pay damages to the purchaser or others for defects in his equipment and accidental damage caused by negligent work while on site. These are:

- Liability under contract – for having supplied equipment or work which is in breach of conditions or warranties under the contract.

- Liability for causing damage or injury to another person through negligence.

- Liability under legislation – there are various statutes that can make the contractor liable for defective work or accidental damage, such as the Occupier's Liability Act (the obligation to make one's premises safe for visitors), the Employer's Liability Act (responsibility for employee insurance against industrial injuries), the Health and Safety at Work Act (HASWA) and so on. These Acts usually do little more than codify existing law. However some legislation does make major changes. By turning industrial accidents into insurance claims the Employer's Liability Act massively reduced litigation costs and the consequences of HASWA have been enormous.

CONTRACTUAL LIABILITY FOR DEFECTS

The original law of commercial contracts was developed by judge-made decisions during the 1800s. That law was then codified in the Sale of Goods Act (1893). Current law is set out in the Unfair Contract Terms Act (1977), the Sale of Goods Act (1979), the Supply of Goods and Services Act (1982), and the Sale and Supply of Goods Act (1994). Again the best way to start is probably by quoting from these Acts.

The Sale of Goods Act (1979) Section 14 (2–3):

(2) Where the seller sells goods in the course of a business, there is an implied condition that the goods supplied under the contract are of merchantable quality, except that there is no such condition –
(a) as regards defects specifically drawn to the buyer's attention before the contract is made; or
(b) if the buyer examines the goods before the contract is made, as regards defects which that examination ought to reveal.

(3) Where the seller sells goods in the cause of a business and the buyer, expressly or by implication, makes known ... to the seller ... any particular purpose for which the goods are being bought, there is an implied condition that the goods supplied under the contract are reasonably fit for that purpose, whether or not that is a purpose for which such goods are commonly supplied, except where the circumstances show that the buyer does not rely, or that it is unreasonable for him to rely, on the skill or judgement of the seller.

The Supply of Goods and Services Act (1982) Section 2 then extended liability under Section 14 of the Sale of Goods Act to 'contracts for the transfer of goods'.

The Sale and Supply of Goods Act (1994) Section 1:

> In section 14 of the Sale of Goods Act 1979 (implied terms about quality or fitness) for subsection 2 there is substituted –
>
> (2) Where the seller sells goods in the course of a business there is an implied term that the goods supplied under the contract are of satisfactory quality.
>
> (2A) For the purposes of this Act, goods are of satisfactory quality if they meet the standard that a reasonable person would regard as satisfactory, taking account of any description of the goods, the price (if relevant) and all the other relevant circumstances.
>
> (2B) For the purposes of this Act, the quality of goods includes their state and condition and the following (among others) are in appropriate cases aspects of the quality of goods –
>
>> (a) fitness for all purposes for which goods of the kind in question are commonly supplied,
>>
>> (b) appearance and finish,
>>
>> (c) freedom from minor defects,
>>
>> (d) safety, and
>>
>> (e) durability.

The Unfair Contract Terms Act (1977) provides several things:

> (2) – (1) A person cannot by reference to any contract term ... exclude or restrict his liability for death or personal injury resulting from negligence.
>
> (2) In the case of other loss or damage, a person cannot so exclude or restrict his liability for negligence except insofar as the term ... satisfies the requirement of reasonableness.
>
> (3) – (1 & 2) (Where one of the contracting parties deals on the other's written standard terms of business) as against that party the other cannot by reference to any contract term –
>
>> (a) when himself in breach of contract, exclude or restrict any liability of his in respect of the breach; or
>>
>> (b) claim to be entitled –
>>
>>> (i) to render a contractual performance substantially different from that which was reasonably expected of him, or
>>>
>>> (ii) in respect of the whole or any part of his contractual obligation to render no performance at all,
>>
> except insofar as (in any of the cases mentioned above in this

subsection) the contract terms satisfies the requirement of reasonableness.

Section 6 then permits, in commercial contracts, the exclusion of exclusion and limitation clauses in respect of Sections 13 and 14 of the Sale of Goods Act 'so far as the term satisfies the requirement of reasonableness'.

And, finally, in Schedule 2 –

The matters to which regard is to be had in particular for the purposes of (defining reasonableness) are any of the following which appear to be relevant –

(a) the strength of the bargaining positions of the parties relative to each other, taking into account (among other things) alternative means by which the customer's requirements could have been met;

(b) whether the customer received any inducement to agree to the term, or in accepting it had an opportunity of entering into a similar contract with other persons but without having to accept a similar term;

(c) whether the customer knew or ought reasonably to have known of the existence and extent of the term (having regard, among other things, to any custom of the trade and any previous course of dealings between the parties);

(d) where the term excludes or restricts any relevant liability if some condition is not complied with, whether it was reasonable at the time of the contract to expect that compliance with that condition would be practicable;

(e) whether the goods were manufactured processed or adapted to the special order of the customer.

This is a real mouthful; but let's take it stage by stage, as a series of statements:

● The Sale of Goods Act lays down the main principles that apply to contracts for the sale of equipment. The Supply of Goods and Services Act then extends virtually identical rules to equipment supplied under other types of contract (such as a construction contract).

● The rules as to defects/quality liability are laid down in Section 14 of the Sale of Goods Act (as amended).

● There are two separate conditions: firstly of 'satisfactory quality', and secondly of 'reasonable fitness for purpose', when the purchaser has made known to the contractor the purpose for which he is buying the equipment, which is usually the case in commercial contracts.

- These conditions apply to all 'goods sold in the course of business'.

- Both the contractor's own equipment and items that he buys in from subcontractors.

- Fitness for purpose implies that the equipment must be capable of use for that purpose; satisfactory quality implies use for normal purposes, value for money, freedom from defects when supplied, defect-free for a reasonable period after supply and so on.

- Obviously there are complex rules concerning exactly what the limits of satisfactory quality and fitness for purpose are, but for our purposes there is no doubt that virtually all manufacturing or selling companies will be squarely within the terms of the Acts. However both these conditions are stated to be 'implied conditions' only that will be implied into a contract unless specifically excluded by the terms of the contract.

- The contractor carries unlimited liability under both the laws of contract and of negligence.

- Liability can be excluded or limited, but only by a clear clause in the contract.

- That clause will only be valid if it is reasonable – see below.

- It is not permissible to try to exclude or limit liability for causing death or injury.

LIABILITY IN TORT (NEGLIGENCE)

The principles of the law of negligence are set out in Chapter 11 below. For the purposes of this chapter note that the law does allow the parties to a contract to agree between them that the right to claim in tort may be excluded, by a clear statement to that effect in the contract.

EXCLUDING AND LIMITING LIABILITY

THE REAL PROBLEM

The problem is money. From the contractor's viewpoint the legal liability/risk for defective products is potentially very serious. He runs a constant risk of a catastrophic consequential loss claim. Obviously in some cases the risk may be somewhat theoretical, but in most major contracts it is not too hard to imagine how the wrong failure at the wrong moment could cause a major accident or loss.

From the purchaser's viewpoint also the situation is far from satisfactory, though the reasons are rather less obvious. These reasons are as follows:

- All that the law says is that equipment must be in good condition when sold. It does not allow the purchaser any after-sales service, and the purchaser's rights to claim from the supplier for equipment that fails some time after sale are far from clear or satisfactory – the purchaser would have to prove that the defect was present in the equipment at the time the equipment was sold (what is usually called a 'latent' defect), and was not caused by his own misuse of the equipment.

- In most cases what the purchaser really needs, and what he really wants as well if equipment breaks down, is to have it put back into working order again as quickly as possible.

- The only way money can be guaranteed to be available to cover a major loss is through insurance.

- Every purchaser will always therefore want a repair/spare parts service and adequate insurance cover. However:
  - Small contractors will only have limited insurance cover.
  - Large contractors will have more insurance cover, but even the largest may well not have enough cover to deal with a major loss.
  - Processing an insurance claim takes a great deal of time, and the time taken increases dramatically if the claim is either large or complicated. Even a simple claim against a single company will take up to a year or more to settle. A complex claim against two or more with a large amount of money at stake can easily take several years to settle. No purchaser wants to wait that long.

Contractors' insurance cover is always a little uncertain. For purchasers the situation is different. When they buy equipment, they buy an asset, and it is easy for the purchaser to take out their own insurance cover on their own assets to the total value of those assets against all risks of loss or damage. Indeed purchasers must have that cover anyway to protect themselves against the risk that one of their own employees might cause a major loss. This insurance cover is both certain from the purchasers' point of view, and considerably cheaper than insurance cover provided by their contractors, and infinitely quicker to produce money in a claim situation.

Therefore, although purchasers are sometimes far from enthusiastic about a situation in which they agree to release a contractor from potential liability, there are fairly strong practical reasons, particularly when complex equipment or equipment which operates in a fairly high-risk area is involved, for the purchaser to release the contractor from liability and rely on his own insurance cover to deal with the risk of a major loss, in return for a 'guarantee' defects repair period from the contractor.

HOW SHOULD AN EXCLUSION OR LIABILITY LIMITATION CLAUSE BE WORDED?

Very carefully indeed – this is one job that is always best left to the experts. If in doubt borrow a clause – don't try to write one for yourself. Adequate exclusion and limitation of liability clauses appear in most model sets of conditions of contract for equipment and work in the electrical, mechanical and process industries or are available through trade associations such as BEAMA, both in relation to defects and accidents on site. Typically an exclusion clause relating to defects will give the purchaser the automatic right to have all defects in the equipment which appear within the guarantee period corrected free of charge by the contractor, but in return it will give the contractor an exclusion of his liability for damages both under the law of contract, particularly under the implied conditions under the Sale of Goods Act and so on, and under the law of tort (except for personal injury or damage caused by negligence). A liability limitation clause will require the contractor to accept full liability for site accidents caused by the contractor up to a monetary limit.

The alternative position, often used in model conditions of contract intended for major contracts, is that of joint insurance cover under which all parties are covered for the results of any damage or site accident, whichever of the parties is actually responsible. Again the principle is to ensure adequate insurance cover without the need for cross-claims between insurers.

THE LEGAL PRINCIPLES

First the rules:

- The law has always been opposed to clauses that can be used to evade legal responsibility.

- This is especially true in consumer protection law. Exclusion or limitation of liability is now banned in consumer contracts.

- Even in commercial contracts the law is still rather unwilling to accept liability avoidance clauses unless it has to. Therefore:
  - The exclusion clause (or limitation clause) must be included in the contract. (You cannot, for example, rely on a notice on site that the contractor does not see until *after* the contract has been signed.)
  - The clause must be clear and precise. Remember what was said in Chapter 7 about contract interpretation. If a clause excludes liability in contract, but not in negligence, the clause will fail.
  - There must be no attempt to avoid liability for causing death or injury to people or causing damage to their own personal property.
  - The clause must pass the test of 'reasonableness'.

– An exclusion clause is intrinsically less reasonable than a limitation clause.

A REASONABLE EXCLUSION CLAUSE

The law on the validity or otherwise of reasonable/unreasonable liability exclusion and limitation clauses in contracts is governed by the Unfair Contract Terms Act (see above). The Act provides that exclusion and limitation clauses in commercial contracts are valid provided that they are reasonable, and then lists some of the factors that will be relevant in deciding whether a clause will be reasonable.

The first rule is that, other things being equal, any exclusion or limitation clause contained in a set of model conditions of contract will probably be reasonable. It would need to be proved, but the law accepts that any set of industry-standard model conditions is trying to reflect the best interests of both sides in the contract and is therefore reflecting a reasonable consensus as to good practice and a fair balance of both parties' interests within that industry.

The second rule is that an exclusion or limitation clause in any other contract, especially where it is based on a set of in-house standard conditions will not be reasonable unless it can be proved that the clause is reasonable.

To prove that the clause is reasonable it has to be shown that the clause formed part of a deal that was reasonable for one party to offer, and for the other to accept. (This is the point of the tests of reasonableness in the Schedule to the Act.)

An example of this is a line of cases, starting with an obiter dictum of Lord Wilberforce in *Photo Production Ltd v Securicor Transport Ltd*. Securicor provided an overnight guarding service to the premises of Photo Production for comparatively low fees. One of Securicor's guards started a fire in the premises which got out of control and caused major damage. The contract was on Securicor standard conditions which excluded their liability for any damage caused to premises which they were guarding. The case began some time before the Unfair Contract Terms Act was passed but reached the House of Lords after the Act had been passed. As a result the Act did not apply, although everybody knew what the Act said by the time the Lords gave judgement. The court decided that the Securicor clause was watertight and therefore Securicor were not liable. However, said Lord Wilberforce, if the same events happened after the Act was in force he would make the same decision, because companies in the modern world manage risk. In risk management terms a clause that says that one party is not responsible often is merely a clause that means that the other party should insure against that loss. Therefore, where both parties could and probably did have the appropriate insurance cover, a clause that said one party would not be liable simply meant that the other should insure. In this case both parties could, and did, have adequate insurance cover. Therefore the clause was purely a risk management clause and perfectly reasonable.

This line of reasoning has been followed in *ICL v St Albans Borough Council* and *Mitchell v Finney Lock Seeds*, and others where it has been accepted that in the commercial contract, exclusion and limitation clauses are often used as a method of risk management in conjunction with insurance. Therefore provided that a reasonable balance is maintained (see *ICL v St Albans*), an exclusion or limitation clause would be valid.

ACCIDENTS

The law is the same in respect of clauses dealing with liability for accidents and damage while working on site. Accidents on site caused by the negligence of the contractor's personnel while carrying out erection, guarantee or other work will cause damage and loss to the purchaser even more surely than defects in the equipment.

The difference between liability for site accidents, in legal terms, is that defects liability can be established either under contract or in negligence (in practice is more easily established in contract than in negligence), whereas site accident liability is almost always dealt with under negligence law. From the viewpoint of the parties involved, however, the insurance argument and considerations are precisely the same – that the risk is best dealt with as a matter for insurance.

IS CIVIL LAW DIFFERENT TO COMMON LAW?

This is a question that cannot be answered in a general way. It is very much a matter of national policy – whether the country decides to allow exclusion of liability or not. Every country allows parties in commercial contracts to limit liability – some also allow parties to exclude liability. German law is very much the same as UK law, for instance, but France only permits the limitation of liability. Most continental countries apply a reasonableness test to liability clauses similar to that in the UK.

This is an area where there is no substitute for good local advice. There are four questions to ask:

- Can I exclude liability or merely limit it?

- Is there any particular form of words that I must use to ensure that my clause will be valid?

- Is there any particular insurance cover that I must have?

- Are there any other requirements or formalities that I must meet?

This last question is very important. Some countries, for instance, require site contractors to be licenced or to have compulsory insurance cover.

CHAPTER 9

The Law of Breach

This chapter sets out the rules relating to contract termination and breach of contract. It then describes the remedies that the injured party has available when a breach has occurred.

CONTRACT TERMINATION

In law contract obligations can be terminated in one of four ways, by

- Agreement
- Performance
- Frustration
- Breach.

AGREEMENT

Many contracts are terminated by bilateral agreement. A contract may be terminated 'for convenience' on an agreed basis when only part-completed, or at the end of the contract when purchaser and contractor sit down together and agree a 'full and final settlement' in which the final payment is agreed, depending upon the various claims and shortcomings of the parties. Sometimes agreement may be not bilateral but unilateral, when a party who has carried out their side of the contract confirms that they accept that the other party has completed its work as well.

PERFORMANCE

By far the largest number of contracts end by performance. Once any party has carried out their contract, their obligations cease. When both parties have done so, the contract ends.

What counts as performance?

The strict common law rule was that only total performance of the whole contract counted as performance. This was soon seen to be impractical and unjust, and the strict rule was relaxed. After all, in the real world, no one ever performs any contract perfectly.

The exceptions to the strict rule are:

- Substantial performance – when a contractor has substantially performed any obligation under the contract or the whole contract, he is entitled to payment of the price, minus a reasonable amount to cover the purchaser's costs of completing the work. (This is easy to apply, say, when a supplier has delivered 98 000 tonnes of coal under a contract to supply 100 000 tonnes, but much more difficult to apply to complex engineering and technology contracts, where substantial performance is virtually the same as complete performance.)

- Partial performance – when the contract has only been partly performed, the purchaser has the option to reject or to retain what has been completed or delivered. If he decides to retain completed work he must pay a reasonable price for what he retains, but can claim damages for everything else.

- Severable performance – where the contract is split into parts (say when equipment is to be installed at a number of totally separate sites), the contractor may be able to claim payment for each consignment as it is installed and any claim for breach would only relate to undelivered consignments.

- Performance prevented – where the purchaser prevents the contractor from performing the contract, the purchase is barred from claiming for breach.

- Acceptance – (under the Sale of Goods Act) when the purchaser has accepted that goods supplied comply with the contract, he then loses the right to reject them.

FRUSTRATION

Very occasionally contracts come to an end through frustration. Under common law this can only happen when (further) performance of the contract has become impossible. An example would be a contract in 1939 to supply equipment between the UK and Germany, which became impossible to perform once war was declared, or an employment contract that ends with the death of the employee. Under civil law the position is that performance must become, not impossible, but almost impossible.

If however performance simply becomes very expensive to one party or of little value to the other the contract is not frustrated. It must be carried out – unless the parties bring it to an end by agreement.

BREACH

Breach of contract is a failure by a party to a contract to carry out any obligation under the contract without a lawful reason/excuse. The normal rule is that the injured party will take action after the breach has occurred.

Do remember that breach can take many different forms and be of many different degrees. It is breach of a contract of sale to refuse to deliver any of the goods at all. It is also breach to deliver only 99 per cent of the goods. It is breach of a contract for the sale of a tonne of copper to deliver a tonne of scrap iron. It is also breach to deliver a tonne of gold or platinum. This is why the injured party is given a range of options. If the contractor indicates a probable minor problem or shortfall to the purchaser well in advance of the completion date the purchaser may very well not want or need to take the drastic step of terminating the contract. He may prefer to make good the shortfall elsewhere.

In addition to straightforward breach there are two types that merit special mention:

- Repudiatory breach – when a party tells the other that he refuses to carry out the contract, or does something which will make it impossible for him to carry out his contract. In that case the injured party can either take immediate action to terminate the contract, or can affirm the contract; in effect take no immediate action but wait to see whether the contract will be performed or not.

- Anticipatory breach – if one party gives advance warning to the other that a breach is going to occur. Say the contractor informs the purchaser several weeks before delivery is due that he will only be able to supply 950 units, instead of 1000. The purchaser now has the right to terminate or affirm the contract. If he affirms the contract he will take delivery of the 950 units in substantial performance of the contract (see also 'Mitigation' below).

Options for the injured party

Because breach can take many forms the injured party has a range of options:

- He can decide to take no action – to affirm the contract or overlook the breach.

- If the other party is in breach of a condition or in serious breach of an innominate term of the contract he can terminate the contract. If that happens then contract obligations on both sides of the contract come to an end and any money paid or work/equipment performed/delivered should be returned (see below), and damages are payable by the party in breach.

- He can claim damages.

- He may also have an equitable remedy available.

Effects of termination by breach

These simply need to be listed:

- The contract comes to an end.

- There is no further performance by either side.

- If the breach is by the contractor then, at the option of the purchaser, goods/equipment may be returned, and the site returned to its former condition.

- All payments will be returned, or reclaimed.

- If the breach is by the purchaser then the contractor may remove equipment from the site.

- Then the injured party is entitled to damages – whatever sum of money is adequate to compensate them for the failure of the other party to carry out the contract (see below.)

REMEDIES FOR BREACH

REMEDIES AVAILABLE

There are two kinds of remedies, automatic common law remedies, which are always available to the injured party, and equitable discretionary remedies, which a court can award to the injured party if the judge thinks it proper to do so. The Common Law remedies are money, damages or payment of the price. The law takes the view that money is almost always an adequate remedy for breach of a commercial contract. Therefore discretionary remedies are only granted occasionally.

The common law remedies are:

- an action to sue for the price (plus interest)

- a claim for damages (plus interest).

The equitable remedies are:

- an injunction

- a specific performance order.

TYPES OF DAMAGES

Damages can be either 'liquidated', agreed by the parties in advance and written into the contract, or 'unliquidated', fixed by a judge or arbitrator and so on. (See Chapter 8 for the principles of liquidated damages.) If the contract includes liquidated damages, that is what is payable. The injured party cannot have both liquidated and unliquidated damages as well.

Unliquidated damages are not limited in amount. The injured party can claim compensation for all loss and damage that results directly from the breach and which at the time of contract the other party could or should reasonably have foreseen would be likely to result from the breach of contract, however great that loss and damage may be.

Unliquidated damages can be *special* or *general*. Say, for example, that there has been an accident while a contractor is working on site. In that accident some equipment has been damaged, and in addition the site has had to be shut down for repairs which has caused a loss of business. The cost of repairing the equipment would be special damages. The purchaser would know exactly what his costs were of carrying out the repair, and would claim those costs back from the contractor. In addition the purchaser would claim general damages from the contractor for his loss of business. He would not be able to prove an exact cost for the loss of business, but he would claim whatever sum he thought appropriate and the judge would then decide what amount to award.

There are two alternative bases for calculating general damages – profit/turnover lost or additional cost/expenditure required. In theory the injured party cannot claim both. In practice most claims contain elements of both.

Proving damages

In theory it is easy. One party is in breach. The injured party can claim in court for all the money he needs to put himself back into the position that he would have been in, if the contract had been carried out properly. What could be more simple?

But damages must be proved. There is a difference between what we know and what we can prove in court. I might know that a particular breach has cost me £100 000. To prove the first £40 000 is easy. To prove the next £30 000 however would become increasingly more difficult. To prove the last £30 000 could be almost impossible, simply because of the difficulty of finding hard evidence, that could not be successfully challenged.

Damages must result directly from the breach. In normal commercial language we talk about 'consequential' liability. The lawyer uses different language: damages are either direct, an immediate consequence of the breach, or are indirect or too remote from the breach to be allowable. There is no fixed line between the two. It is up to the judge to decide.

The loss must be foreseeable. There are two types of foreseeable loss. First, the party in breach will be automatically liable for damages in respect of all types of loss that any reasonable person would foresee as likely to arise from the breach of contract that actually occurred. Second, he will also be liable for damages in respect of any further types of loss that he had been warned about by the purchaser before the contract was signed. As an example, one classic case concerned delay in carrying out a contract for the supply of additional boiler capacity to a dyeing works. The purchaser intended to use the additional capacity to carry out lucrative contracts to dye cloth for the Ministry of Defence. Because the boiler was late the purchaser lost the contracts. However the purchaser had not told the contractor about them. As a result the purchaser was only permitted damages for the loss of normally foreseeable business profits – with no allowance for the profit it would actually have made on the Ministry contracts.

Mitigation

Mitigation is the duty to 'soften the blow'. Every injured party must take whatever action he can to keep any claim for damages down to a reasonably low sum.

EQUITABLE REMEDIES

They are only available to parties who have dealt fairly with the other side, and they will only be allowed in special circumstances. They are:

- Injunction – an order by the court not to do it again – often used to prevent further breach, for example of a confidentiality clause or a licence agreement. Used in addition to a claim for damages for the breach that has already happened. Claimants may sometimes ask for an interim injunction – asking the judge to order the other side not to do something until it has been decided whether they have the right to do so or not.

- Specific Performance Order – an order of the court to carry out the contract – only used where the injured party needs the work done and the other party is almost literally the only one who can do it.

Failure to comply with the terms of an injunction or specific performance order is contempt of court for which the offender may be fined or imprisoned, and still then required to comply.

LIMITATION PERIOD

If a claimant wishes to take legal action he must commence that action within the limitation period. This starts when the work under the contract is complete. In a contract for the supply of services that would be when the services are completed. In a contract for the supply/installation of equipment that would be when handover takes place and the defects repair/guarantee period commences. The limitation period is six years.

CIVIL LAW COUNTRIES

THE POSITION IN CIVIL LAW

Compensation for breach of contract or of the law of obligations is always going to be very much a matter of national policy. Therefore there are differences between the UK approach and those of other countries, although every country will aim to do the same thing – compensate the injured party.

In commercial contracts civil law systems take much the same position as English law. Performance also discharges the parties from their obligations under the contract. French law takes the same position as English law on substantial performance and part performance. German law is similar; German law also operates a similar doctrine to English law in respect of anticipatory breach. French law does not recognise anticipatory breach at least in theory.

One difference already noted between English law and civil law is that under English law where one party is in breach of a condition (or innominate term) of the contract the other can terminate the contract. Under civil law systems the injured party cannot do so unless the contract specifically includes a clause that gives him the power to terminate. Instead he must apply to the court for the court to order termination. Commercial contracts in civil law countries therefore tend to include a termination clause as a matter of course – so that the injured party can avoid the time and expense of having to go to court. This is a very good example of how we write contracts differently under different legal systems so that we can achieve the same practical result.

FRUSTRATION

The concept of frustration of contract is unknown to civil law. Instead it operates a system based upon *force majeure*, the intervention of something outside the control of a party which raises an insuperable obstacle to the execution of the contract, or which makes it so economically difficult to perform that it would not be in good faith to demand performance. This is perhaps a rather more liberal rule than the doctrine of frustration, but is equally seldom applied.

REMEDIES

Most civil law systems provide similar remedies to common law. However they adopt a more generous view of damages for breach than English law. Both French and German law would allow damages covering all the direct losses resulting from the breach whether foreseeable or not, whereas the English rule is much more restrictive. In addition French law is much more prepared to order specific performance than either English or German law.

PART IV

Involving the Experts

Most of the time we can run our contracts without needing to use any expertise from outside the company. Occasionally we do need outside help.

This can happen in two situations: when we need assistance in doing something correctly; and when something has gone wrong, possibly badly wrong, and we have no choice but to call in the professional specialist to sort out the problem.

This part looks at the issues when we have to do this.

CHAPTER 10

Using the Professionals

> This chapter sets out the considerations to bear in mind when approaching the lawyers and others for advice and assistance.

THE RULES

Most of the time you will *not* need outside advice provided that you comply with a few basic rules. Remember that a large part of any contract only matters when the contract goes wrong. The basic rules are:

1. Equip yourself with good sets of contract conditions.
   Sometimes this is easier said than done. But every company, whether a purchaser or contractor, needs to have standard conditions of contract that are appropriate to what it actually does. Needs vary from company to company. One company may simply need sets of small-print conditions on the reverse of its sales and purchase stationery. Another might need small-print conditions, plus small contract conditions, plus large contract conditions. Another might need separate conditions for supply, hire and servicing contracts and so on. Advice on getting good sets of contract conditions is always worthwhile.

2. If you also use model contract conditions, then use the appropriate ones – for obvious reasons.

3. Make sure that you understand what they say.
   This means two things. The company must know what the conditions say, and everyone who uses the conditions must know what they say. This requires training/familiarisation of some kind. For a contractor training should cover at least the commercial, sales, estimating, tendering and contract management, and for a purchaser at least the engineering/ design procurement and project management functions.

4. Start from that basis.
   We may not always use our own preferred conditions, but if we know what they say we have a standard of comparison to use when looking at other conditions.

5. Understand the contract specification.
    More contracts have problems because of mistakes and misunder-
    standings in this area than for all other reasons put together.

6. Understand who is supposed to do what.

7. Understand what is included in the price.

8. Understand the procedures for dealing with change.
    Change is almost inevitable. Understanding the rules in the contract for
    managing change is important to the smooth running of the project.

9. Run the contract in accordance with the rules.

10. Keep good records.
    Because if you do happen to get into a dispute, what matters is not what
    you know but what you can prove.

FINDING ADVICE

The basic rule is that an hour of advice before we are in trouble is worth many hours
after trouble has started.

There are several different categories of advice and assistance to consider:

- advice on commercial matters, such as market intelligence, insurance,
  export or import requirements and procedures;

- advice and assistance in putting the contract together, writing the contract
  conditions, preparing designs and specifications and other documents;

- advice on contract law and contract interpretation;

- advice and assistance in dealing with contract problems or claims; and

- advice and assistance in dealing with formal disputes procedures, litigation,
  arbitration and so on.

ORGANISATIONS OFFERING ADVICE AND ASSISTANCE

First let us deal with a preliminary point. Information is available from many sources.
Government is often very willing to provide advice. National government departments
and overseas embassies will help where they can. Sometimes local government
departments can provide help. Then there is a whole series of other organisations that
may help. Trade associations, chambers of trade and commerce, the CBI, universities
and many others will help with information or by directing you to others who do have
the information. Engineering institutions, the EU, the Internet, creditworthiness
organisations (such as Dun & Bradstreet) – the list is almost endless.

Advice and assistance are a different matter. Broadly speaking they come principally from three different industries: the legal industry, the consulting industry and the claims industry (all of which can also provide information). The basic thing to remember about the people who work in these industries is that everyone is expert in something – but no one is expert in everything.

The legal industry is made up of solicitors and barristers. Obviously both solicitors and barristers are fully competent to advise on matters of law. However this statement must be qualified. The legal industry is made up of specialist worlds. A lawyer who specialises in tax law or criminal law may not be very expert in matters of contract law or contract conditions.

Within the UK the vast majority of barristers work primarily as single individuals, grouped within chambers. Their principal function is to act as advocates. As such they are expert in court procedure, and the preparation and presentation of cases in court on behalf of their clients. Many barristers are also highly expert in particular areas of law. Some are even expert in a particular industry. Sometimes barristers will advise clients, but this is comparatively rare.

Solicitors usually work as single practitioners, when they will rarely handle commercial contract matters, or as members of partnerships. Partnerships can be of almost any size, from two or three up to hundreds of members in size. As a rough rule of thumb small partnerships are unlikely to have much expertise in dealing with large commercial project contracts. Larger partnerships are more likely to include individuals and departments with the appropriate specialist knowledge. Always look for the partnership with a department of experts. Solicitors are experts in procedures and in handling large quantities of documentation.

The consulting industry is made up of everything from enormous partnerships of international consultants and consulting engineers with hundreds of specialists in many different areas, down to single individual consultants.

The claims industry is a branch of one part of the consulting industry, specifically aimed at helping clients to deal with contentious matters and disputes arising out of contracts. They provide expertise in formulating claims or defences to claims and like solicitors can provide resources to deal with the inevitable masses of paper that are involved.

CHOOSING AN ADVISER

When you need advice you should probably look for the following:

- experience

- theoretical knowledge

- practical knowledge

- track record.

They are not the same, though they often overlap. They must all be relevant to your own industry and problem. Remember that every external adviser has expertise to offer. The problem is whether or not that expertise is appropriate and useful to you.

The basic thing to remember is that any outside adviser understands the area in which they are experts. What they do not understand is the client's business or problems. However much they may understand in general terms, there will always be a lot about you that they do not know. Therefore whenever you go to an outside adviser the first thing that you have to do is decide:

- exactly what questions you want to ask;

- what assistance you may need; and

- what you need to tell them

so that they understand what you are asking them to do.

In general terms this means that you need to prepare a brief for the adviser before you see them. The brief should cover the business that you are in, the contract/project that you want to discuss, the particular problem on which you need advice and so on. If you are consulting an adviser about a problem on an existing contract you also need to prepare a statement setting out precisely what has happened during the contract, so that they can see right from the start where you are.

Sources of advice

- Commercial advice – generally speaking the best source of advice is the consulting industry.

- Putting the contract together – the consulting industry can usually provide both advice and assistance in preparing both the technical and contract/commercial parts of the contract. The legal industry and claims industry can also provide advice and assistance in preparing the contract/commercial parts of the contract.

- Contract meaning – from all three industries.

- Contract problems – from all three industries.

- Contract disputes – generally speaking from within the legal industry and the claims industry. Always remember however that these two industries earn their living from dispute. Remember, too, that disagreement is normal and healthy. Dispute is not.

What are the pitfalls? There's many a slip … There are far too many to list. The simple rule is that in a formal dispute you need a good case, and you must get everything right. Any mistake might lose you the dispute.

CHAPTER 11

Disputes

This chapter explains the principal methods for resolving a dispute that are available within the UK and elsewhere. It then looks at the advantages and disadvantages that go with each of them.

FAIRNESS IN LAW

The first thing to understand is that the law is not fair when it comes to using legal methods to resolve a dispute. Of course every judge, arbitrator or adjudicator will want to be fair if they can – but that is not the point. A tribunal has to decide the dispute according to the evidence, and if the evidence is not there, they have no choice. The law is just – which is a very different thing. It gives each side the equal opportunity to prove its case. The side that does so will win.

Therefore if you are going to win a legal dispute you have to have several things. First of all you have to have a good case. Secondly you have to have the evidence to prove your case, and to cast enough doubt on your opponent's case. Then you have to comply with the procedures. If you can do all these you will probably win, most of the time.

METHODS OF RESOLVING DISPUTES

The best method of solving any dispute arising out of a contract is negotiation. It will be much quicker, much less costly in terms of money and man-hours, and will probably produce a more equitable solution than any other method. It is also far less likely to cause damage to the commercial relationship. The problem is that negotiation requires willingness on both sides to compromise and admit one's own mistakes.

If negotiation is not an option, or has been tried and failed, then the options are, in order of degree of legal formality:

- expert determination
- alternative dispute resolution (ADR)

- adjudication

- arbitration

- litigation.

Broadly speaking the greater the degree of legal formality involved, the longer the process takes and the greater the cost to both sides. There are exceptions. Adjudication is probably the quickest of all methods, though more expensive than expert determination or ADR. Expert determination and ADR are about equal in time and cost, depending upon the size/complexity of the dispute.

EXPERT DETERMINATION

Potentially, at least, expert determination is the least formal method. It is used in the process industry, where it is very successful, and has wider applications as well. It requires usually a clause in the contract stating that certain disputes are to be settled by an expert. The dispute in question will usually be technical/factual, as opposed to legal/contractual. It might be about the interpretation of engineering data, the cost of variation work or what would be a reasonable time to carry out a variation.

The principle is very simple. A dispute has arisen. The parties will appoint an independent person who is an expert in the area of the dispute. If they cannot agree then a third-party appointing body, such as the Institution of Chemical Engineers, will make the appointment. They will then each present their side of the argument to the expert. The expert will hear both the parties out and give them the opportunity to comment upon each other's arguments. Then the expert will consider the problem, make whatever additional enquiries he feels are necessary, and give them his decision. That decision binds the parties. There is no appeal (unless of course the expert has acted wilfully or fraudulently).

The expert will decide his own procedure, and the parties will usually make their presentations to him, without the need to use professional lawyers, though sometimes they may employ lawyers or consultants if they wish. Whatever procedure the expert chooses to adopt he will usually be expected to conform to the rules of 'natural justice'. Essentially these are that:

- both sides should be treated in the same way;

- each side should be allowed to put its own case, verbally and/or in writing;

- each side should hear/see the other side's case;

- each side should be allowed the opportunity to comment upon the other side's case; and

- the expert should make his decision after giving due consideration to what both sides have put to him.

The expert is usually appointed because of his:

- ability to be impartial;

- ability to manage the dispute; and

- expertise in the area of the dispute.

He is expected to use that expertise in making his decision, unlike a judge or arbitrator who will make his decision solely on the basis of the evidence and arguments put to him by the parties.

The process will usually be that the expert will call the parties to a preliminary meeting at which a timetable is set for the parties to present their cases to the expert, and to each other, usually in writing. From then on procedure depends on the nature of the dispute. The expert may interview/question the parties separately or together. He may hold a hearing or he may not. The process is flexible. The overall timescale is perhaps 3–6 months and the cost is low. The process is confidential. Almost any dispute can be dealt with in this way, but the process lends itself to the settlement of straightforward disputes relating to facts, rather than disputes involving complex legal or contractual issues.

Another example of this method of dispute resolution is what is sometimes called the 'look-see' arbitration, often used in the valuation of goods, for example, in the shipping industry. The point is that it it is quick, inexpensive, and it is decisive. This helps to prevent disputes. There certainly seems to be a considerable amount of anecdotal evidence in the process industry that people avoid disputes because they don't want to have those disputes referred to an expert.

ALTERNATIVE DISPUTE RESOLUTION

The next group of methods that needs to be considered is what is called alternative dispute resolution. These ideas again have been around for some considerable time but there has been a great increase in interest in them in recent years as a result of significant success in the USA. Usually, though it is not a requirement, they will result from contracts that include an ADR clause.

Essentially ADR procedures are methods of resolving disagreements that avoid using legal procedure or lawyers to reach a settlement. They take the form of structured formalised negotiations under the guidance of an expert in the procedure. They are optional and consensual, in that they rely upon the goodwill of the parties, and their being prepared to adopt these methods. If either of the parties is unwilling to go down the ADR route then ADR cannot take place. They are preliminary procedures, in the sense that if successful they settle the matter and no formal dispute will happen. However if the parties are unwilling or ADR fails then formal dispute procedures can then take over.

The two basic procedures are 'conciliation/mediation' and the 'mini-trial'. The terms mediation and conciliation are used almost interchangeably in some senses.

What happens in the first of these is that the parties will agree to appoint someone (or maybe sometimes two persons) as a conciliator or mediator. He will then familiarise himself with the cases of both parties, maybe sit down with each of the parties in turn and go through their case to ensure that he understands what the salient points of that case are. He may also comment to each party upon the strength of its case, and suggest possible areas of compromise.

Then he will conduct an intensive process of 'shuttle-diplomacy' moving between the two parties, passing on proposals and arguments and comments from each party to the other, and balancing concessions between them. He will also introduce suggestions of his own for possible ways of finding a compromise, and generally do all that he can to negotiate both of the parties towards a mutually acceptable settlement. The final stage may well be a meeting of both parties under his chairmanship. Hopefully this will result in the parties reaching a settlement of the dispute.The process may take a day, or maybe several days.

The difference between conciliation and mediation is a narrow one. A conciliator is rather like a marriage broker, in that his task is to help the parties find their own solution. Mediation follows much the same lines as conciliation, but a mediator would take a rather stronger line than a conciliator in pushing the parties towards whatever solution he himself feels to be equitable – remembering that the outsider can often see things that the insider cannot.

The parties may use lawyers or consultants to help with the presentation of their case if they wish.

Conciliation/mediation is worthwhile. Perhaps conciliation is a better method of solving a complex dispute, while mediation is better for simpler disputes. Both methods work well if there is goodwill.

The mini-trial is a more formal procedure but again works on a basis of goodwill. Representatives of each side, usually a manager, present their case to an informal tribunal comprising senior management from both companies, under the chairmanship of an independent person. The decision of the tribunal decides the dispute.

A variation of the process that one sees in major projects is the 'dispute resolution board', set up as a permanent mini-trial tribunal.

The basic advantages of all these methods are that they get the issues out into the open, so that they can be talked through quickly and with outside assistance. The overall time-scale is perhaps 2–4 months, the cost is low and the process is confidential.

ADJUDICATION

Adjudication is a high-speed arbitration process with very few rules. It was created by the Housing Grants Construction and Regeneration Act 1996 primarily to provide small contractors in the civil engineering and building industries with a means to achieve at least a quick interim settlement of their claims. Under the Act, adjudication must be available in any dispute in a 'construction contract'. (It may also be applied in other contracts by agreement of the parties.) Essentially a construction contract is a contract concerned with building construction or demolition work on site. The right to adjudication overlays any other rights under the contract. It must be completed within a basic period of four weeks after the adjudicator's appointment, which may be extended to six weeks with the claimant's agreement. The decision of the adjudicator binds the parties, subject to any re-hearing of the dispute in arbitration or litigation.

Often contract conditions will require preliminary procedures to define the dispute before adjudication can begin. The purpose of this is to ensure that the process does not begin until the points at issue have been clearly identified. Experience has already shown that where the dispute is complicated there is a much greater chance of success if the precise nature of the dispute is clear before the adjudication process begins. If it is not clear the adjudicator will waste precious time identifying the issues.

The process begins with the appointment of the adjudicator, by agreement of the parties or by nomination by an accredited appointing body, and his agreement to accept the appointment. Normally the adjudicator will know the approximate nature of the dispute by his appointment . Usually he will immediately write to the parties giving them instructions for the conduct of the adjudication. There will be a preliminary stage comprising the submission to him in writing of their statements of claims and/or counterclaims by each party. The rest is up to the adjudicator. He can decide his own procedure. He may decide to visit the site; he may hold hearings with the parties jointly or separately; may question witnesses, or ask to see documents; can impose time limits on the parties and proceed with the adjudication even if the parties fail to meet those time limits. Then he will give his decision in writing usually setting out the reasons for that decision.

The decision of the adjudicator will then stand unless it is reversed by arbitration or litigation. Litigation/arbitration is not an appeal against the adjudicator's decision, but a complete re-hearing of the dispute.

The procedure is essentially legalistic and parties usually choose to use lawyers or consultants to assist in the preparation and presentation of their cases.

When applied in the right circumstances adjudication is a common sense remedy that works. The only difficulty is that a good adjudicator will probably be fairly busy. He will have commitments and appointments to meet. If he has to solve a dispute within four weeks of being notified of the dispute, he will not have much time. If the dispute is simple so that only a few days are needed to consider the evidence and make a decision then the adjudicator will be able to make a high quality decision. If the dispute is large or complex involving masses of documentation and complicated arguments, and many disputes in building and construction work can be complicated, then the adjudicator's decision may be of slightly less high quality. This is always the risk when under time pressure. Quality must suffer when the system is over-loaded.

The courts have already shown themselves to be very supportive of adjudication, (as they are of expert determination). The classic way for a defendant to try to avoid being taken to adjudication is to object to the adjudicator or to his jurisdiction to decide the dispute. Unless very well founded indeed, objections are almost always dismissed by the courts. Furthermore the courts have shown themselves to be supportive of adjudicators when complaints have been made about the procedures that they have followed. Naturally, however, the courts have from time to time overruled the decisions made by adjudicators – but then no one is perfect.

ARBITRATION

Arbitration as a method of solving commercial disputes has been around for a very long time. The decision will be made by an arbitrator, not by a judge. The parties can select an arbitrator who has a much greater understanding of the technology and the industry than any judge can ever have. Proceedings do not take place in public in the intimidating surroundings of a court, but in private.

Also when properly conducted arbitration is undoubtedly rather more efficient in commercial disputes than litigation. An arbitrator would generally reckon to get a dispute sorted out in approximately half the time that litigation would take – or less. Reducing the required time reduces legal fees. Arbitrators have considerable powers to decide the way in which any arbitration should be run, precisely for the purpose of keeping the duration and cost down.

The other advantage of arbitration is that it is much more confidential than litigation, which takes place in open court. In court competitors can listen to the parties washing their dirty linen in public. This cannot happen in arbitration. The only publicity is if a decision is appealed, and even then it is minimal.

The problem is that arbitration is still to some extent tied to the law. Costs follow success in just the same way that they do in litigation. Almost inevitably the parties will use lawyers to prepare their case and present the case to the arbitrator. Certainly they do in commercial disputes. So arbitration in effect cannot be totally divorced from litigation. It is different but it is related.

The process requires an 'arbitration agreement', usually a clause in the contract stating that disputes should be settled by arbitration. Appointment of the arbitrator will usually be by agreement between the parties, or if there is no agreement, then by an appointing body named in the contract. The arbitrator will not accept the appointment unless satisfied on two points, firstly that he has no conflict of interest and secondly that the dispute is one that he is properly qualified to decide.

The process begins with the arbitrator holding a preliminary meeting at which he gives the parties instructions as to how the arbitration is to proceed. This will normally entail a preliminary stage during which the parties will exchange information in writing about their cases. This can be done in two ways, either by 'pleadings', or by 'statements of case'.

Pleadings have their roots in litigation. The judge is a busy person. He does not have time to read masses of documentation before the case begins. Therefore what he wants is to see a set of documents at the start of the court hearings which will tell him what each party is going to prove. This is what pleadings are designed to do. The aim is to end up with a series of statements that a judge can understand setting out what facts the claimant intends to prove, and what facts the defendant intends to prove in reply. The judge then listens to the barristers do their work in court and decides what the result of the case is by applying the law to the facts that they have proved. It is up to the advocates for each side to decide how they are going to prove their facts, by producing witnesses to give evidence in court or by producing documentary evidence.

The other method of exchanging information, which is more usually used in arbitration, is that of statements of case. A statement of case is a document that sets

out what the party claims, what facts it relies on for that claim and what evidence it has
to support the claim that it is making.

Once pleadings or statements of case are completed there will then be a 'disclosure
of documents' stage when each party is given access to the other party's documents
relating to the dispute. This stage is of course very important because it enables both
parties, to some extent or even to a considerable extent, to check the truth of what the
other party is claiming.

Then the parties will prepare for a hearing, and the hearing will take place. At the
hearing both sides will present their evidence to the arbitrator, usually with the help of
an advocate. Witnesses will be examined, cross-examined and re-examined, the
advocates will make open and closing statements and the arbitrator will issue a written
decision.

Arbitration can also be done on a documents-only basis. This is a much shorter and
simpler form, carried out on the basis of detailed statements of case. Both sides will
produce statements and then be given the opportunity to comment on the other side's
statement. The arbitrator will then issue his decision on the basis of the documents.

Appeals against an arbitrator's decision go to the High Court/Court of Appeal/
House of Lords, on matters of law, only.

The advantages of arbitration are clear. It provides a legal route to dispute
resolution that has several advantages over litigation. It takes one-half to one-third of
the time. It is confidential. It will cost perhaps one half of the cost of litigation. The
arbitrator may be a lawyer, or he may be an expert in the field in which the arbitration
takes place. As a result his technical decision may be better than that of the judge who
is not usually an expert.

Against this, arbitration has several disadvantages. It is procedural and litigious in
the same way that litigation is. It is still expensive. The parties usually have to employ,
in practice even if not necessarily in theory, solicitors and barristers. Producing
evidence in front of an arbitrator is just as much a lottery as producing evidence in
front of the judge. If the arbitrator does not believe the witness, the case can be lost
even if it should not be lost. In addition there is the problem of producing witnesses to
give evidence when the hearing takes place (see below).

LITIGATION

Going to litigation was the traditional method of dealing with disputes that could not
be settled in any other way. Unfortunately in the modern world this means the full
panoply and expense of the law. The problem is that lawyers are the most expensive

sub-contractors in the world. The judge and court come free, unlike an arbitrator who has to be paid for. However everyone else has to be paid for. A senior solicitor will cost anything up to £2–3000 per day. A junior barrister will cost anything up to £5000 a day. If you use a QC then you will have both a junior at up to £5000 a day and a QC at anything up to £10 000 a day.

The law is very efficient at straightforward matters, such as claiming an unpaid debt. However as soon as a dispute arises about the facts or the law, litigation becomes slow, difficult and very expensive. A typical commercial dispute in the High Court may well take two or three years before it reaches court. It can easily cost well over £100–200 000 in lawyer's fees for each side (to which must be added say another £50 000 each in internal support costs), and the outcome may well be uncertain. This problem of uncertainty is made worse by the principle that the loser pays the costs. The best way of explaining the problem is by taking an example.

You and I are in a serious legal dispute. We are each claiming a substantial sum from the other. At the end of the case the judge finds that we have both proved that some of our claims are justified. He awards you damages of £450 000 against me and me £440 000 against you. This means that you have won. I now have to pay you £10 000 in damages, plus interest on the money. However we might each have spent say £300 000 in legal fees on the dispute, together with internal costs of £100 000. As I have lost I have to meet all my own costs. In addition I have to pay your costs. However in practice I will not be responsible for all your costs. Your actual costs would be vetted by a court official who would decide how much I should actually pay, on the basis that I should only have to reimburse the cost of the litigation, not the costs of general advice. This will result in an award of approximately two-thirds of the actual legal costs that you have incurred. As a result the case would cost me £10 000 (damages), plus £400 000 (my own costs), plus £225 000 (your costs), a total of £635 000. The case would cost you £175 000 (your costs), less £10 000, a total of £165 000. BUT YOU WOULD HAVE WON!

In the 1940s and 1950s almost every commercial dispute in the UK went to litigation; however it has become increasingly clear over the years that legal procedure is so slow and complex that it is an increasing uneconomic and inefficient way to settle disputes. (One particular element that causes an incredible amount of cost is that the modern project creates so much paperwork, all of which has to be read by at least two lawyers on both sides.) As a result for something like 30–40 years in the UK there has been a steady movement against using litigation to settle commercial disputes. This has resulted in moves towards arbitration and then towards the other dispute resolution procedures outlined above. Indeed the judges themselves regularly insist that the parties try to mediate a dispute before coming to court.

The process is similar to that for arbitration. It begins with a preliminary hearing with the judge setting timescales for pleadings. The timescales will be generous and there may be several stages of pleadings before the process is complete. Then a disclosure stage will follow, and after that both sides will prepare the case for the court hearings. There may then be a long wait for a court hearing. The problem is that judges are busy people and a complex commercial case with large amounts of documentation to be dealt with might well require three or four weeks court time. The parties may well have to wait for many months before the judge, barristers and so on all have the same three or four weeks clear in their diaries.

When the hearing takes place the advocates will make an opening speech then the claimant will present their case. This will be managed by the advocate. He will present documentary evidence to the court and then witnesses will give evidence, and be cross-examined and re-examined. Giving evidence in open court before a judge can be a very unnerving experience for witnesses. I myself have seen a witness giving evidence in court being so affected by the pressure that he answered a question No when he meant to say Yes. As a result the other side lost the case and we won. We did not deserve to win, but we did.

Once evidence has been given for the claimant the defendant will then present his evidence in the same way. The advocates will then make closing speeches to the judge and the judge will make his decision. Costs follow success in the same way as for arbitration.

There is no appeal from the decision of the judge as to what the facts are. If the judge decides to believe the evidence of one witness and not to believe the evidence of another witness that is entirely his prerogative. If however either party believes that in giving his decision the judge got the law wrong then there is appeal to the Court of Appeal and perhaps then to the House of Lords.

The advantages of litigation are that the company has its day in court. It will get a high quality legal decision on the dispute. If it wins it gets a high-profile victory. The disadvantages are many.

Of course there are the Small Claims Court and the County Court, which are efficient, quick and inexpensive, but most commercial claims are too large to be dealt with anywhere but the High Court. Every company going to the High Court in a case where the facts are complex and disputed must expect to spend a lot in getting the decision, and if the case goes to appeal, £50 000 a time in going to the Court of Appeal and/or the House of Lords. The duration of any case will be at least two years (on average) and may be considerably longer. The personnel involved with the original contract may find themselves tied up for anything up to 50 per cent of their time for the entire duration of the case. Giving evidence in an open court is washing one's dirty linen in public. Anyone can listen to the evidence if they wish.

Finally there is always a particular problem in high-technology disputes. The theory is that 'expert evidence' or 'evidence of opinion', as opposed to evidence of fact, must be given to the court by 'expert witnesses' who are qualified to express an independent opinion on the technology questions involved. Expert witnesses are presumed to be independent of the parties and unbiased in the evidence they give to the court. In practice of course if the claimant retains an expert witness to support its case the defendant will retain another expert witness to do precisely the opposite. It then it becomes very difficult to be certain which of the expert witnesses the judge will actually believe. (This is true of arbitration as well, though an expert arbitrator is less likely to be misled.)

OTHER COUNTRIES

Broadly speaking these procedures will be available everywhere else in the world. But this is an area where any UK company must take local advice, and must have local lawyers to represent it. With a proper clause written into the contract expert determination procedures will be available in most countries, unless domestic legislation would view the procedure as usurping the right to go to law – since there is no appeal from the expert's decision. ADR will always be available.

Adjudication, as a form of high-speed arbitration created by statute and peculiar to one type of contract in one industry, is special to the UK construction industry but other countries might have similar procedures available under their own legal systems. However this depends on the individual country.

Litigation and arbitration are available in every country in the world. Generally speaking common law countries will follow UK procedure. However every single country will have its own particular laws and rules which decide how they operate. There is therefore no substitute for high quality local advice if you are involved in dispute resolution procedures in any other country.

Two last comments should be made.

First the problem of expert evidence is usually handled differently in civil law countries. The precise procedure will vary, but typically the court will appoint an independent expert as adviser to the court. He will hold a preliminary meeting with both parties and their expert witnesses to go through their technical evidence. He will then prepare a report to the judge. That report will state whether the court expert finds in favour of the claimant or defendant and why, as well as summarising and explaining their technical evidence in terms that the judge can understand. That report is also given to the parties. If either or both parties wish they can then submit their own technical reports to the judge criticising or commenting on the report of the court expert. (I have to say that this system does work well, probably better than the UK system.)

Second the basic principle upon which the common law litigation/arbitration system operates (other than for documents-only arbitration) is that 'witness', as opposed to documentary, evidence should be given by the witnesses making oral statements in court so that they can be cross-examined by the advocate for the other side. Common law lawyers will always say this is a considerable advantage that common law gives the judge or arbitrator because advocates are skilled at demonstrating when a witness is not telling the whole truth. This therefore improves the quality of the decision. Oral evidence is a key feature in all common law countries.

In a civil law country the system is very different. Obviously the system varies from country to country but there is a much higher reliance on the presentation of all evidence in writing. In effect cases are decided not on the basis of witnesses giving evidence in the witness box but on the basis of sworn statements made by witnesses and submitted to the judge. The advocates may well address the court on matters of law, but not on evidence. I have been involved in litigation in France and Germany and I have to say that the quality of decision in both those countries is just as high as the quality of decision within the UK.

Undoubtedly advocates in the UK are very good at demonstrating to the court or arbitrator when a witness is not telling the truth. To that extent common lawyers are correct. Unfortunately common law advocates are also very good at attacking the credibility of witnesses when those witnesses are telling the truth, but the truth that they are telling is not the truth that the advocate wants the judge or arbitrator to believe.

Additionally in the normal commercial dispute witnesses are being asked to give evidence about events that may have occurred several years earlier. Memory can be a very fragile thing under the pressures of the witness box, and sworn statements by truthful witnesses made much nearer the event and without pressure can often be much more accurate.

PREPARING FOR A DISPUTE

THE STEPS TO TAKE

- Decide which dispute method you intend to use.
  Different methods impose different requirements on the parties.

- Get your case in order.

- Before disagreement becomes dispute, take a good hard look at your case. Have you carried out your side of the contract properly? If not, then why not? What has the other side done that you do not like? Is this a breach of contract – or not? If it is a breach then why have they done it? Is it because of something that you have done or failed to do? And have you raised objections to their breach – or have you just let them go ahead? (Condoning or accepting a breach may prevent you from challenging that breach later.)

- Organise your advice and assistance.
  First get outside advice on the strengths and weaknesses of your case. Then you will need assistance in preparing the case. Dispute almost inevitably involves organising and collating all the project paperwork to support the case that you wish to make. This needs large quantities of specialist skilled manhours, which usually have to be bought in from the claims or legal industry.

- Organise your dispute team.
  In theory it is just possible for organisations to be represented in litigation adjudication or arbitration by an employee without any legal qualification. (For instance this can happen in litigation with the consent of the judge.) However in practice this is usually done by the legal industry, or possibly, especially in adjudication, by the claims industry. Get the team organised and ready.

- Be prepared to bite the bullet.
  Dispute professionals, legal or otherwise are expensive, and often very expensive.

- Organise your management team.
  A dispute is a project, and like any other project it needs managing. The legal and claims industries are hard to manage. They work on a day-rate basis, off-site, and it is extremely difficult to see what they are actually doing day-by-day. All too often therefore companies allow themselves to be managed by the dispute team, rather than taking control. Every dispute project needs a manager with sufficient power/authority and understanding of the issues to be able to control the dispute, and a 'dispute sponsor' to represent the dispute at senior management or board level.

- Organise your evidence.
  Can you produce the evidence to prove your case? If you need to prove that a particular point was agreed at a particular meeting and no minutes of the meeting were made how are you going to prove it? Is it referred to in correspondence by the other side? Is it referred to in file notes? If you need to

prove it by asking the people who were present at the meeting to give evidence, do they remember clearly and will they make good witnesses? Also are they still available? If the two people present at the meeting were made redundant three months later and are now working for one of your competitors on projects in Japan and Sri Lanka you have a serious problem, and it is better to face it right at the start.

Using the law to deal with disputes

The law is good at some things. If people don't pay their bills the law gives an effective and efficient remedy (usually). However the legal process is not good at dispute resolution. Therefore only resort to law when there is no better alternative, and only when you need to make a point, whatever the cost, or when the amount at stake is high enough to justify that cost.

When NOT to use the law

In addition to what has been said above, don't use the law when you do not have a case, when other alternatives are available, or when you don't want to destroy your commercial relationship with the other side. Going through any dispute can be a very bruising experience for both parties.

PART V

Liability Law

The law of contract is concerned with the responsibility of the parties to a contract to carry out their obligations to each other properly.

However the company is not just liable to people or other organisations when it has a contract with them. It is also liable to them if it causes them loss damage or injury in some way that is wrongful in the eyes of the law.

This part therefore is concerned with explaining the ways in which the company can be liable to the rest of society, or certainly those parts of the rest of society that are in the line of fire, if the company makes a bad mistake.

CHAPTER 12

Negligence

If the company is going to be liable to others it will usually be in one of two ways. The first is for breach of contract. The second is in tort, usually for causing accidental loss or damage and usually in negligence. This chapter sets out the principles of negligence law and liability.

THE LAW OF TORT

A tort is a wrong. (Remember your French – 'J'ai tort' means 'I am wrong'.) It means causing damage or injury to someone else without any legal excuse and in circumstances where it is proper that the injured party should get some compensation for his loss. For instance defamation, libel and slander, is a tort. So is trespass to land, causing damage to someone's property, which is also usually a crime as well. There are several others: deceit (fraud), assault, conspiracy, nuisance and so on. By far the most common tort, and the most important in commercial terms is negligence.

WHY NEGLIGENCE IS SO IMPORTANT COMMERCIALLY

Claims in tort account for 85 per cent of all civil litigation in the UK. All but a few of these claims are for damages for negligence, and the vast majority are against companies. More and more negligence is used as the basis for compensation claims against companies.

THE PRINCIPLES OF LIABILITY FOR NEGLIGENCE

If any person (or organisation) can reasonably foresee that his actions could cause damage or injury to another if done negligently or recklessly then he owes a duty to that person to take reasonable care not to cause him that type of injury or damage by his actions.

The principles are best explained by giving examples:

- When I drive a car along a road I can foresee that I could cause damage to other road users. If therefore I drive negligently and cause an accident, as a result of which another road user suffers damage or injury, then I am in breach of my duty of care to that other road user who may therefore claim damages from me.

- If I am making equipment I can see that I could cause damage to people who will use that equipment. And so on.

Everything is based on foresight, that is whom we should foresee as being in proximity to us, and then what consequences we can (or a reasonable person would) reasonably foresee as a result of our actions. We are basically liable to people whom we can foresee as likely to be damaged or injured for the damage or injury that we can foresee is likely to occur. There is no need to prove deliberate intention to injure or damage other people. Indeed the usual situation is that the defendant was trying not to cause injury or damage, but failed.

WHERE DOES THE LAW COME FROM?

Negligence is very much 'judge-made' law. There was no law of negligence at all in the UK until the principles were laid down in a landmark case in 1932, *Donoghue v Stevenson*, which was almost the first consumer protection/product liability case.

The facts were that a young lady suffered severe food poisoning from drinking ginger beer from a bottle containing a putrefied snail. (They knew it had been a snail because of the shell – the only recognisable bit left.) The bottle had been returned to the manufacturer and was not cleaned properly before being re-filled and re-sold. The bottle was bought for her by a friend in a snack bar. The result was that no-one could claim damages under the law of contract (under Sections 13 and 14 of the Sale of Goods Act). The buyer could not claim damages as she had not been injured, and the victim could not claim damages either because she was not the buyer. She therefore decided to sue the manufacturer, David Stevenson. The case went to the Lords, who had clearly decided that the time had come to establish a basis for liability under common law for culpable injury/damage caused by a failure to take reasonable care.

The leading judgement was given by Lord Atkin. He said 'You must take reasonable care to avoid acts or omissions which you can reasonably foresee would be likely to injure … persons who are so closely and directly affected by your acts that you ought reasonably to have them in mind when you are considering the acts or omissions in question.'

The principles that the case laid down were:

- Reasonable – if I, as a reasonable person/organisation
- Foresight – can foresee the risk of damage or injury to

- Victim – any other person or organisation who is likely to be affected by what I do or fail to do, then

- Duty of care – I owe him/her/it an obligation to take reasonable care, and if

- Failure – I then fail to take reasonable care

- Damage or injury – and as a result I do cause damage or injury

- Type – of the types that were foreseeable

- Victim – to any person to whom I do owe a duty

- Liability – then I am liable to compensate that victim for all the damage or injury that I have caused

- Extent – however much it costs to do so.

Of course terminology changes over the years. In 1932 Lord Atkin defined the potential victim as someone who was reasonably foreseeable as being likely to be affected by a negligent act. In later cases the courts have restated the law by defining the principles of liability on the basis of the causal 'proximity' of the parties to each other, rather than foreseeability. There is no substantial difference between the two.

Donoghue v Stevenson let a very large cat out of the bag. The principles of negligence spread to accidents at work, and on the roads, to consumer protection cases, to medical and professional negligence and so on. Now they can be applied to almost all activities – so that the courts are now worrying about just how far negligence liability should be allowed to go, and academic argument rages on the point. But if from a practical viewpoint you are trying to identify in advance the possible situations where you might incur liability, so that you can take the appropriate avoidance action where necessary there is no problem. Just assume the worst. Everything you do could create potential liabilty to someone.

A REASONABLE MAN

The standard or level of foresight required by the law is generally described as that of the 'reasonable man'. Judges have described him as the man who goes home by public transport after work, or the man who does the garden on Saturday afternoon. However this is a fairly elastic concept. Where we are dealing with the average member of the public the law does not demand a high level of foresight, unless he has special skills. If the person has more than average knowledge or specialist skill then the law expects him to use that skill or knowledge. The more expert you are in any field, the more likely you are to be able to foresee the risks, and therefore the more likely you are to owe others a duty of care as a result. The professional, car mechanic, doctor or whatever is always going to have a greater degree of foresight than the amateur. They are expected to know what is dangerous. The commercial organisation is *always* expected to be expert in its business areas. After all it employs professionals, and is expected to know what they know.

REASONABLE CARE

The level of care that is to be expected of the average reasonable man. But this can be elastic as well. In certain situations even the average reasonable man is expected to take a very high level of care. For example everyone is expected to show a high level of care, or skill in other words, when they drive a car – and the same high standard is expected of a young athlete and an old age pensioner. Usually however the ordinary person is not expected to show any exceptional level of skill.

But, when the actual person is an expert he is expected to show the level of care/skill of the average expert, not the level of care/skill of the average non-expert. The organisation is always expert.

In one case, in 1947, an anaesthetist gave an injection to a patient in accordance with the established procedure at that time. The patient suffered serious injury, and as a result of the incident an investigation was carried out which showed that there was a serious flaw in the established procedure for sterilising needles. The procedure was changed. In 1954 the patient sued the hospital for damages, claiming that, as investigation had shown that the 1947 procedure was wrong, the anaesthetist was negligent in following that procedure. The judge dismissed the claim. He said that if the anaesthetist in 1947 was acting as any good anaesthetist would in 1947 then he was not negligent. In other words the level of care/skill is that level of care or skill which is thought appropriate at the time, even if that level is later known to be wrong.

But (and in law there is always a 'but') the problem is that in the world of technology the judge always looks at an incident with the benefit of several years hindsight, and with the benefit of forensic examination which often shows precisely what went wrong. He can therefore identify which party did it wrong. If the party that did it wrong was an organisation that is expert, it is often only a very small step to say that if the organisation was expert and did something wrong then the organisation should have foreseen that doing it wrong might have consequences.

CAUSATION

The failure to take care must cause the loss or damage. This has a number of aspects. If someone is negligent but that negligence causes no damage then there is no liability. If for instance I crash my car into a wall but the wall is not damaged, I have no liability to the owner of the wall. If I am negligent and someone else is also negligent then we will both be liable to the victim for a share of the damages. If I am negligent and the victim is also negligent then my liability will be reduced by his 'contributory negligence'. (Remember the cases a few years ago when damages were reduced in car accident cases because the injured had not been wearing seatbelts.) If I set in motion an 'inevitable chain of causation' then I am liable. In one case someone threw a lighted firework into a crowd. It landed on someone who instinctively threw it away from him. This happened again. Then the firework exploded and someone was injured. The original thrower was found liable to the eventual victim. The two people in between were found not liable. They were acting out of self-preservation.

TYPES OF LOSS OR DAMAGE

We are liable for the types that were foreseeable. If I break your leg in a car accident I am liable to compensate you for the injury because it is injury of a type that is foreseeable.

In one case sparks from welding operations on a ship set fire to oil floating on the water beside the ship. The fire spread and seriously damaged a wharf nearby. The technical evidence was that no one would expect floating oil to catch fire. (The reason why it actually did catch fire was that floating wood or waste acted as a wick.) The welding company had checked and been told that the oil would not catch fire. They were therefore not negligent. The company that had negligently spilled the oil knew that it could cause pollution, but did not know that it could cause a fire. They were therefore also held not liable for the fire damage. The loss was held to be an accident, and no one's fault.

EXTENT OF DAMAGE

We are liable for the whole extent. We have to take our victim as we find him. If a victim is more vulnerable to the injury or damage that we cause, that is our problem not his. In one case a minor industrial accident caused a small burn. The burn re-activated a dormant tumour, causing the death of the victim. The employer was found liable.

In addition we are liable for all the consequences that follow the loss/damage, so far as those consequences are reasonably foreseeable. If I break your leg in a car accident, I can foresee the physical injury to you, damage to the clothes you are wearing, your loss of earnings while you recover, and the fact that the injury might have some permanent effect upon your future earning capacity. If it just so happens that you are a rising star soloist with the Bolshoi ballet, that is my bad luck.

In a commercial context, if I cause an accident in your factory which puts machinery out of action for three months and costs you millions in lost profit, that is my bad luck as well.

ORGANISATION OR COMPANY LIABILITY

The company is liable for the actions of its employees. The partnership is liable for the actions of its partners and its employees.

This liability is called 'vicarious' liability. It is liability for the acts of employees when those employees are doing the work for which they were employed. This is true even if the employee was actually disobeying his or her instructions. It is true if the employee was acting 'for his own convenience'. It is true even if the employee was actually committing a criminal act. In one case an employee of a firm of solicitors, as a part of his work, visited clients of the firm to get papers signed by them. The employee visited a client and manipulated the client into signing certificates transferring the ownership of the client's shares to himself. He then sold the shares and disappeared with the proceeds. The firm was held liable because, although its employee had been wilfully disobeying instructions for the purposes of fraud, he had still been carrying out actions which were part of his normal work.

Who is an employee?

Most employees will be employees because they are on the payroll. However many other people may also fall into the category of employees for the purposes of negligence liability. There are a number of tests to decide whether or not non-employed people are actually employees of the organisation.

One test is whether or not the organisation has the power to control what the person does. Another is the power to control how he does it. In one case a company hired out a crane complete with driver. The terms of hire were that the driver would obey the instructions given to him by the customers. When he injured someone the crane owner was liable. The customers could tell the driver what they wanted the crane to do, but the owner could tell the driver how to drive the crane.

Another test is whether or not the person is a 'member of the team'. In one case a surgeon carrying out operations in a hospital was held to be an employee of the hospital for the purposes of negligence liability. The surgeon was self-employed and was in complete control of what he did. No-one else was entitled to give him instructions during an operation. Nevertheless the hospital was liable because the surgeon was an integral part of the hospital's operating team.

Another test is simply to look at all the facts to see whether on an overall view the individual is an employee, for which the organisation is liable, or is merely a sub-contractor for which the organisation is not liable.

What does a victim have to prove?

The 'burden of proof' is on the victim. He has to show that he was within causal proximity to the defendant, that the defendant failed to take reasonable care, and that as a result of that failure he suffered injury or damage of a type that could be foreseen. (This is different to the position in contract where the claimant simply has to prove that the defendant failed to carry out the terms of the contract and that as a direct result the claimant suffered loss.) The victim is then entitled to damages, whatever sum of money will compensate him for the damage/injury that he has suffered and the financial and other consequences of the damage/injury, (pain/suffering, loss of earnings, continuing medical care and so on). The hard part is sometimes proving causal proximity. Liability in the tobacco industry is a case in point.

Liability in negligence is usually only for physical damage or injury plus its consequences, both physical and economic (but see below).

In one situation the burden of proof can be reversed. In one case a passer-by in the street was injured when a heavy sack filled with sugar fell out of the open doorway of an upper floor of a warehouse. The passer-by could prove that the sack fell and that he was injured, but he could not show how the sack came to fall. The warehouse owners defended themselves on the basis that if the victim could not show how the sack had fallen then there was no liability. The judge however said that there were three probable reasons why the sack might have fallen. It might have been stacked badly. One of the employees of the warehouse might have pushed it. A trespasser might have been allowed access to the warehouse and pushed it. In all these cases, said the judge, the warehouse owners were liable. In a situation where all the probable causes of the incident were the responsibility of the defendants then it was the responsibility of the defendants to prove that they were not negligent, rather than the responsibility of the victim to prove that the defendants were negligent. This principle is known by the tag *res ipsa loquitur* – the facts speak for themselves.

LIMITATION PERIOD

The victim must take action within the limitation period. This starts when the injury or damage becomes apparent, not when the tort is committed. (This is one of the reasons why Lloyds was in so much trouble a few years ago. It was being haunted by asbestosis claims resulting from actions by its policy-holders many years before the disease actually developed.) As a result liability in tort can last for many years after any liability under a contract has ended. (The limitation period for breach of contract commences when the contract work is complete.) The limitation period is six years where the claim is in respect of damage to property, but only three years in the case of personal injury.

DEFENCES TO A CLAIM

There is a whole series of defences to claims in negligence that may apply. They are fairly straightforward:

- consent – normal injuries – on the sports field, for example. Whenever we go for dental treatment we are asked to sign a consent form.

- normal life – bumping into someone in the street.

- accident – and therefore unintentional. A car accident caused by oil spilled on the road, or because a driver had suffered a heart attack at the wheel (and see above).

- act of God

- legality – the act was authorised by law.

- necessity – injuring someone while rescuing them, for example.

- self-defence

- mistake

- act of a third party

- inspection – if the victim had taken the usual precautions to be expected of any normal person.

LIABILITY FOR PSYCHOLOGICAL INJURY

This is a difficult area. The law is that you are liable if as a reasonable person you can foresee the likelihood of causing injury. However once someone is in the line of fire you must take your victims as you find them. The problem is that some victims are abnormally sensitive, or are put under exceptional stress. The courts have always shied away from holding claimants liable where their actions have caused mental trauma rather than physical trauma (because lawyers feel uncomfortable without clear proof – a broken arm is easy). It is now however accepted that there are a number of cases in which the court will find claimants liable for the physical consequences and costs of non-physical trauma.

There are three situations where this occurs:

- when the victim is a woman who is pregnant, when the normal hormonal balance changes;

- when we are worried for the safety of our immediate family, or even property; and

- where a rescuer has suffered trauma, post-traumatic stress disorder (PTSD) as it is now known, as the result of his experiences while carrying out a rescue under harrowing circumstances.

The classic example of this in recent years was the Hillsborough disaster. Some members of the police service and others working to rescue the injured and recover the bodies of the dead received damages for PTSD. Relatives inside the ground and outside the ground recovered damages for Nervous Shock. (Relatives who merely saw pictures on television news programmes did not. The court held that they were not in sufficient proximity to the disaster, perhaps feeling that as a matter of policy a line had to be drawn somewhere.)

LIABILITY FOR GIVING NEGLIGENT ADVICE

First you can be liable if you give negligent advice that causes physical injury or damage. Secondly you can also be liable in very specific circumstances if you give advice that causes no physical damage but only causes economic loss. Normally there is no liability in negligence for causing economic harm unless at the same time we have caused physical injury or damage. Liability can exist if the following factors are present:

- The advice must be given negligently.
  This means that the giver of the advice has recklessly or negligently failed to check whether his advice was true or not. Essentially this means that the giver of the advice could have checked the facts and didn't, or failed to think carefully before he gave the advice.

- The advice must be wrong.
  Sometimes of course advice is merely a question of opinion. 'Given that there are two equally attractive alternatives my advice would be to do A rather than B' is probably not actionable, simply because a choice between two equal alternatives is not wrong. However if the advice is based on wrong information or given thoughtlessly then the advice may be actionable. Of course, if I get my facts wrong, but still give you the right advice then I am in the clear.

- The advice must be given with the intention to persuade or the knowledge that it will persuade.

- The advice must actually persuade and be acted on.
  Here there is a problem for the company. Advice, for example by a stockbroker to invest in the shares of a particular company to a private individual might persuade. The same advice to a company might not persuade. The company would be expected to use its own expertise to check for itself before deciding what to do.

- There must be a relationship of dependence between the giver of the advice and the victim.
  (This is where proximity arises.) It must be reasonable for the giver of the advice to assume that the victim is relying on him for the advice and will act on that advice – and that if that advice is wrong the victim will suffer loss as a result.

- The victim must suffer loss.

- The loss may be purely financial/economic.

This kind of negligence liability is a comparatively recent development. It originally developed in cases dealing with financial advice, but has spread to legal advice and technical and engineering advice, for example whether a second-hand car was a good buy.

CAN LEGISLATION MAKE ME LIABLE

Yes. Sometimes legislation will impose liability in negligence. This can happen especially when an area of negligence law is codified. Examples are employer's liability, road traffic accidents, pollution and so on.

One special area is the liability of the occupiers of premises: under The Occupier's Liability Act 1984, 'a ... duty of care to all lawful visitors to the premises' plus the duty to warn of hidden risks and dangers even to trespassers, and the duty to take all reasonable steps to try to protect children against injury. Children are a special case. If adults want to risk life and limb playing with something dangerous after they have been given due warning that is up to them. However simple warning notices will not deter children. Therefore the act requires the occupier to take reasonable precautions to prevent children playing with dangerous things on his land or premises.

LIABILITY FOR THE ACTS OF CONTRACTORS OR SUBCONTRACTORS

The company is not usually liable for the negligence of its independent contractors or subcontractors, except in special circumstances. These are:-

- where a hazard has been created on a highway (public road/footpath and so on);

- exceptionally risky operations, say testing new drugs;

- where a personal duty is involved; and

- perhaps where there is very clear negligence in contractor selection.

CIVIL LAW

The civil law theory is different. English law has lots of separate torts – defamation, trespass, negligence and so on. Civil law approaches the problem of civil liability for injury, termed 'delict', from a completely general position.

French law states simply 'Every act whatever of man which causes damage to another obliges that person by whose fault it occurred to make good the damage.' No duty of care is necessary. Therefore liability could be much wider than under UK law.

German law provides three grounds for an action in tort: first an overall liability similar to French law, second the infringement of a statute intended to protect others, and third the intentional causing of damage to another in a manner contrary to public policy.

The terms of both French and German law are therefore similar and obviously extremely vague. What really matters is how these principles have been applied in practice, in other words by looking at the decisions made by the courts. This is how the UK operates as well. There is a generic similarity between all these systems – whether it is the common law or civil law, tort/delict law tends to be judge-made, and judges think in similar ways.

BASIS OF LIABILITY

Civil law liability for delict/tort depends on fault. Fault includes both intentional and negligent conduct that causes damage. Under French law fault is an act deserving of 'moral reprobation'. The courts then apply a totally objective standard to when an act is deserving of moral reprobation, which is in practice almost identical to the common law definition of the 'reasonable man'. German law defines negligence as a failure to use the requisite standard of care in dealing with others. The standard is defined as that which would be considered 'proper in the circumstances by ordinary prudent persons'. In effect both French and German law adopt a similar approach to that of English law.

DUTY OF CARE

Common law requires there to be a 'duty of care' based upon proximity for there to be liability for negligent damage or injury. French law does not require any duty for liability to exist. The French civil code sets out a 'general duty' not to injure others. In other words a negligent act creates a much wider potential liability under French law than under common law. (To give a practical example it might be much easier under French law for a cancer sufferer to sue a tobacco company for damages than it would be in the UK or the USA. Almost all the cases against the tobacco industry in the USA have failed because the claimants have failed to show that the tobacco companies owed them a duty of care.)

German law again adopts a different approach. It lists various types of interest that are protected against negligent infringement and then imposes a general principle that anyone who creates a hazard is automatically liable for injury caused by it (compare *Rylands v Fletcher*, see Chapter 13). This is perhaps not too far removed from the position under common law.

German law is much closer to UK law in theory and practice than French law; but in practice in commercial claim situations French law is not much different.

LIABILITY FOR EMPLOYEES

The French approach to the question of the vicarious liability of an employer for the acts of his employees is virtually identical to English law.

German law adopts a different position. Under German law the employer is only liable for the acts of his employees where he is himself at fault, by either failing to exercise proper care in the selection or training of his employees or to supervise them properly, or failing to supply the proper tools and so on. He is not liable if proper care by him would not have, or did not, prevent the damage.

This obviously reduces the vicarious liability of the employer under German law, especially for a fraudulent employee, but the position regarding damage caused by a negligent employee, especially if the employee has been negligent before, is broadly similar. And, after all, almost any normal accident will be due to or contributed by a failure by the organisation to supervise or train employees.

CHAPTER 13

Liability for Escapes

> This chapter summarises other areas of law that we need to bear in mind when working on site or operating facilities on a site.

CORPORATE AND PERSONAL LIABILITY

We said in Chapter 12 that the law of negligence had become a major factor in the liability, or potential liability, of companies. There are several other areas of law that need to be understood as well if the picture is to be complete, especially in relation to what we do on site. The difficulty is that they tend to overlap. But just remember that the idea is that a person can do anything he likes on his own land, provided that it does not cause a problem for his neighbours, but if he causes problems for his neighbours by allowing anything to 'escape' from his land on to theirs, he is then responsible for the damage he has caused. This basic principle is then complemented by three others: the introduction of planning laws, which automatically allow particular areas to be used for industrial purposes; environmental protection and control of pollution; and finally the use of criminal law to control companies. As a result there are four strands to current law.

A VAST AMOUNT OF LAW

There is another problem. Put very simply there is now an awful lot of law that we need to obey. It is impossible in a book like this even to try to summarise this law. All we can do is to draw attention to the problem. It can be demonstrated by two simple statements:

- In 1995 a book was published simply listing and describing the then current Health and Safety laws/regulations in force in the UK. It ran to 600 pages. Most of the modern UK legislation implements the requirements of eight major EU Directives (1989–1993). The current key legislation is five major Regulations all issued in 1992 and operative in full by January 1997 (under the authority of the Health and Safety at Work Act).

- A summary of the current environmental protection and pollution law provisions within the UK would have to cover no less than twelve major Acts of Parliament, numberless minor references in other legislation, over 80

European Union Directives, nearly one hundred major UK Statutory
Instruments, and many smaller items of delegated legislation.

It is stating the obvious, but every other country within the EU will be in much the
same position. Again there is no substitute for good local advice.

CRIMINAL LAW COMES INTO THE PICTURE

In a speech to the European Parliament as long ago as the early 1980s Jacques Delors
said that governments throughout the European Union were generally agreed that one
of the major problems facing them was how to control industrial companies.
Increasingly, he said, governments were turning towards the use of criminal law
directly applicable to directors and managers to do so.

This has continued. There has been a steady increase over the last 25 years in the
powers of government to control industry and commerce through the use of criminal
law, directed against managers, executives and engineers.

There are several main areas that affect project industries (there are others as well,
in the area of consumer protection for instance):

- fraudulent/wrongful trading – company directors

- environmental protection – directors, managers and staff

- health and safety at work – directors, managers and staff

- public safety – directors, managers and staff directly involved in any incident
  (with hesitant moves towards corporate manslaughter)

- pollution liability – directors, managers and staff.

The principle of almost all of this legislation is that in the event of any incident the
'enforcement authorities' in local/national government may investigate the incident
and then prosecute any organisation and any individual who they believe to be
culpable. The usual penalty is fines, but other penalties such as imprisonment or
disqualification as a director are also possible in some cases. Again these trends are
Europe-wide.

Environment protection and pollution legislation in the UK alone has created 110,
at the last count, separate punishable criminal offences. Also remember that almost all
of this legislation also permits civil claims by injured parties in addition to any fines or
other punishment. Please be warned.

STRICT LIABILITY

LIABILITY FOR CREATING A HAZARD/ESCAPE

This goes back to the famous case of *Rylands v Fletcher*. The owner of a mill built a dam to create a reservoir to store water to drive his mill wheel. At the bottom of the new reservoir there were old mine workings. The mill owner therefore employed a contractor to block up the shafts. Unfortunately the contractor's work was inadequate. As a result when the reservoir was filled with water the water penetrated the shafts and flooded a coal mine on neighbouring land. The owner of the mine sued the mill owner for the loss of his mine – and won. The mill owner had not been negligent. He had behaved perfectly properly. He was liable because he had created a hazard. He had collected on his land a large amount of water, which was likely to cause damage to neighbouring properties if it escaped. It did escape. Therefore he was responsible for the damage caused by the hazard that he himself had created whether he was negligent or not.

Note that this is liability between the owner/user of land and his neighbour for damage to land and premises. Escapes law is becoming more important in a pollution-conscious age. Rylands liability can apply to water, chemicals, pollutants, explosions, gases, wild animals (in zoos) and so on – any situation where there is a foreseeable risk of damage to neighbouring property, and how often do we store hazardous or dangerous items or materials on site?

NUISANCE LIABILITY

PUBLIC NUISANCE

This can be very quickly dealt with. It is a crime, and covers a multitude of sins: such things as a badly-organised pop festival, obstructing the highway, throwing fireworks, selling food which is unfit for human consumption and running a brothel. The only reason why it is mentioned here is that anyone who has suffered particular damage because of a public nuisance is entitled to claim damages. A classic example of this occurred when the GLC built a ferry terminal on the Thames close to a sugar refinery at Silvertown in East London. The terminal caused silting up of the riverbed and interfered with the ability of the sugar refinery to bring ships up the river to its dock. It was held that this was a public nuisance and that as the sugar refinery had suffered particular damage they were entitled to bring an action for public nuisance and claim damages for the cost of dredging.

PRIVATE NUISANCE

This is the unlawful interference with use or enjoyment of land. Essentially it consists of doing something, continuously or on a regular basis which unduly interferes with someone else's use of their property. Typical examples are creating smoke, effluent and smells. To be unlawful the conduct of the defendant must be 'unreasonable'. For example, unless there is a smoke control by-law in place everyone in a residential area might expect their next-door neighbour to have the occasional bonfire in his or her garden. That is perfectly reasonable. However it would not be reasonable to use a bonfire to burn car tyres three times a week. What is reasonable depends upon the locality, whether the act is useful or not, malicious or not, and so on. The claimant is entitled to damages, plus possibly an injunction to restrain any repeat of the nuisance.

PLANNING LEGISLATION

Of course, where commercial and manufacturing activities are concerned, the law has been radically changed by the introduction in the UK of planning legislation. Previously to that the commercial enterprise was always liable to an action in private nuisance on the basis that what they were doing was unreasonable. Planning legislation changes all that, simply by giving permission to commercial organisations to carry on normal manufacturing and commercial activities in certain areas. Essentially this means that these activities, and the automatic results of those activities cannot constitute a nuisance when carried out in areas where planning permission has been given for those activities to be carried out.

POLLUTION LEGISLATION

Finally under Part II of the Environmental Protection Act 1990 it is an offence to deposit waste on land or to allow any premises to deteriorate to the point where they become likely to cause damage to the environment or harm to human health. In the event that this happens the local authority is entitled to serve an order, what is called an 'abatement notice', on the owner of the premises/land requiring him essentially to put the site into good order. If he then fails to do so the authority can take whatever action is necessary to put the site into good order, and then claim the costs of doing so from the owner. In addition any person who is particularly aggrieved by the problem is entitled to claim compensation. This compensation however would be calculated on a comparatively restricted basis, so that in serious cases the aggrieved party might well wish to take action in private nuisance, which would allow him much greater damages plus an injunction. Abatement notices can be served in case of premises becoming a nuisance, being prejudicial to health, emitting smoke fumes or gases, having an accumulation of waste materials or contamination, and so on.

PART VI

Other Important Topics

This final part deals with a selection of topics that regularly give rise to serious misunderstandings among managers and engineers.

As with everything else in this book, the rules are actually quite simple once they are explained.

CHAPTER 14

Intellectual Property

This chapter deals with the methods by which the company can protect its most valuable, and usually undervalued, asset – its knowledge.

INTRODUCTION

Intellectual property is a term used to describe a group of legal rights to the ownership of innovation information or trading position. They give us the power to stop others using our knowledge or goodwill, at least to some extent. They matter because they help to protect assets of the organisation that are always vulnerable. Information and knowledge in particular can be given away too easily by being passed across an interface. Projects and contracts are made up of interfaces, between design personnel, site personnel, management personnel and so on. If the interfaces are not managed correctly valuable information will be given away. Once it has gone it can never be recovered.

Remember, too, that this is an area where law is usually fairly similar in most countries, but is far from being identical.

Intellectual property rights create a monopoly. Government, whether national government or at the level of the European Union, dislikes monopolies because they restrict freedom of trade. Therefore government has to balance its interest in scientific and technological development, which is encouraged by intellectual property rights in the results of that development, against its interest in promoting free trade. Therefore the overall position on intellectual property rights represents an uneasy compromise. The basic rule is that provided you follow the rules laid down by government precisely then you will get your monopoly for a limited period of time. If you fail to comply with the rules then you lose your monopoly.

TYPES OF INTELLECTUAL PROPERTY

There are four types of intellectual property that protect innovation. These are, the patent, the registered design, the design right, and copyright. In addition we also need to consider knowhow.

Trade marks and trade names protect market position, or goodwill. They are outside the scope of this book.

Patents and registered designs are both created by a formal inspection and registration process (administered by the Patent Office). The other types are informal, but there is still a need to be able to prove creation in the case of design right or copyright, or knowledge in the case of knowhow.

All types of intellectual property are expensive to police and enforce. Enforcement action usually means two things: a claim for damages covering lost income, plus an injunction to prevent further abuse. All types of intellectual property come complete with implied licences (see below).

THE PATENT

In the UK, as in most countries 'things' can be patented but 'ideas', scientific principles or discoveries cannot. For example the laws of nuclear physics cannot be patented, but a nuclear reactor, which applies those principles, might be. Also, except in very special circumstances, computer programmes cannot be patented. (There is a particular problem with the USA, which has allowed patents to be granted for 'discoveries', such as DNA, and also for computer software.)

Patents valid within the UK can be granted by two organisations: the UK Patent Office in London/Gwent, which grants a patent within the UK, and the EU Patent Office in Munich, which will grant a patent valid within several EU countries.

A MONOPOLY RIGHT

A patent is a monopoly right granted by the state to the inventor of a new 'invention', in return for the disclosure of that invention to the public at large in the patent document, so that anyone can use the idea after the monopoly comes to an end. To qualify the invention must be a new device, a new process for making something, a new combination of devices, or a new use for an existing device. It must be an *inventive* step – something that could not be developed in the normal run. Once something has been invented it cannot be re-invented. It is part of existing knowledge, what is sometimes called 'prior art'. Therefore in most areas of technology, where people have been inventing new things for many years, only a small percentage of the developments that we make will qualify as inventions. Most developments, however valuable they may be, will not qualify. The exceptions are areas of new technology that are still at a comparatively early stage of development, and industries such as pharmaceuticals, where every drug is different.

The patent itself is a published document, on sale within the country where it is granted. It will state what the invention is, and what is new about it. It will also describe how to make the invention work. Of course this description will usually be in very elliptical language. The inventor will not want it to be too easy for the competition to work out what he has done. Usual UK practice is to employ patent agents, professional experts in intellectual property law procedure and drafting.

A patent must be applied for as soon as the invention has been made, or at any rate before it becomes public knowledge. It must be applied for within the country where the invention was made (or at the EU Patent Office, if made within the EU). This is usually a preliminary application, which must be followed within a year by a final application. The application process is slow, involving detailed checks to confirm that the invention is not anticipated by any prior art, and patents are expensive to obtain and to maintain. Once granted the patent will last for up to around 20 years, depending upon the country concerned (20 years in the UK) and provided that annual renewal fees for the patent are paid.

The owner has exclusive rights to use and control the use by others of the patented invention during the life of the patent, and can take legal action for infringement by any unauthorised user. The owner may also sell and licence the patent to others. Once the initial patent has been granted the owner may, if he wishes, apply for similar patents in other countries (under the terms of the Vienna Convention).

PRIORITY DATE

Patents are granted on a first-come-first-served and winner-takes-all basis. The first inventor gets the patent, and no-one else gets anything. In the UK, as in most countries, the first inventor is the first person to submit an application, usually the preliminary application. However the USA does it differently with the date of 'discovery', not the date of application, deciding priority.

INVENTIONS MADE BY AN EMPLOYEE

In the UK the basic right to apply for any patent lies with its human inventor(s), who will then own that patent when granted. In certain circumstances however the rights to the patent, when granted, will belong to the employer. This can happen in three ways:

- where an employee who is also a director of the company makes an invention that relates to the business of the company;

- where the employee is 'employed to invent', in a research or development role for instance; or

- where any other employee makes an invention 'in the course of his normal duties', which is however rare. It would be unusual for any normal employee outside a research or development department to have making inventions as a part of his job description, unless he had (say) been given the job of finding the answer to a very specific problem.

IMPLIED LICENCES

The sale/purchase/supply of any patented device carries with it the right for the purchaser to use the equipment for all normal purposes and to do everything necessary to keep it in running order. This right is in the form of an implied licence under the patent. It includes rights to operate and maintain, and also to repair the equipment and to have it repaired by others, including the right to make and have made 'Chinese copies' as spare parts.

The implied licence will transfer to any further owner of the equipment. It will not include any rights to make copies of the equipment to give away to others or to sell for profit.

DESIGN RIGHTS

Under the Copyright, Designs and Patents Act 1988 there are two separate rights that may exist in a design, meaning a three-dimensional shape. (In addition, of course, the design will be put into the form of a drawing, which will be protected by copyright, see below. Some designs can also even be trade marks – the design of the Coca-Cola bottle is the most famous example.)

First there is the registered design. A design may be registered at the Patents Office on payment of a fee. Protection lasts for a maximum of 25 years from registration, with renewal fees payable every five years. Registered designs are usually used to protect an industrial design with some artistic merit, usually in the consumer goods field. They are designs of things. There could be a registered design relating to a coffee percolator for instance, but not to the design on wallpaper or a carpet (which is copyright).

Secondly, the design of any new article or thing is protected against copying by a 'design right' which comes into being at the date on which the drawing is first made. The design date must be proved usually by keeping the original drawing signed by the draughtsman and dated. There is no need for registration. Protection will last for a period of either 10 years from the end of the first year when the equipment is sold or 15 years from the date of the design, whichever is the shorter. The design right covers the shape and configuration of the whole and any part of the article, and allows the owner of the design right to prevent copying by others, (but not 'Chinese copying' to make spare parts).

Both registered designs and design rights may be bought, sold and licenced.

Registered designs belong to the person who registers them. Design rights belong to the person who caused them to be produced. In other words if I place a contract for a subcontractor to prepare a design for me, the design right will belong to me, provided the contract is properly worded. (However the copyright might still belong to the subcontractor, unless the contract requires the subcontractor to give me that as well.) In general terms all designs drawn by any employee in the course of his normal work belong to the employer. Any other designs will belong to the employee.

Essentially there are similar implied licences to those that apply to patented equipment.

COPYRIGHT

Copyright is simply a right of protection against copying all or a recognisable part (see below) of something that has required skill and labour to write or draw. It was originally developed to protect artistic or literary works, so that it protected music, drama, poetry, drawings and so on. Now it applies to commercial material as well. It covers all written documents, drawings, computer programmes and circuit drawings in permanent form. It is not registerable, but belongs automatically to the creator of the copyright article. It protects the content of the document (the actual words, drawings and so on used) and the way that content is set out. The owner has the right to prevent others copying, to grant licences and to sell the copyright. It lasts for 70 years, within the EU.

A recognisable part does not need to be a large part, so long as it can be recognised. A paragraph could easily be a recognisable part of a book, for example.

Often documents are marked with a copyright mark '©' followed by the name of the owner. This is not essential under UK law, but it is useful as it identifies the owner and reminds any user that the owner expects their copyright to be respected. (Note the copyright notices on page iv of this book, by the way.)

In general terms the copyright in all things written or drawn, including computer software, by employee in the course of their normal work belong to the employer. Anything done outside their normal work will belong to the employee.

The sale/purchase/supply of any copyright item carries with it the implied licence to make reasonable use of the item within the business and to make reasonable copies of all or part of it for those purposes. The licence does not include any right to make copies of the item for resale, or for use to make commercial profit.

KNOWHOW

Knowhow is simply knowledge, knowledge about something or of how to do something. We often think of knowhow only in terms of engineering or technology knowhow, but the term includes a much wider range of knowledge. Every organisation has knowhow in marketing, procurement, commercial as well as technical knowledge. Much of that knowhow will be common to many, but every company will use its knowhow in making its products and carrying out its business.

There is no intellectual property right in knowhow. As a judge once said, there cannot be a monopoly in knowledge. For example anyone who knows that two plus two equals four is free to use that knowledge to do arithmetic. Knowledge of how to manufacture a computer is no different, in legal terms, to knowing how to do arithmetic. Therefore knowhow can only be protected in two ways:

- by keeping it secret, or

- by protection by contractual methods, confidentiality clauses and agreements,

or a judicious combination of both.

There are no implied licences in knowhow.

KNOWHOW DEVELOPED BY AN EMPLOYEE

In general terms the employee will have the right to use whatever he knows. If he is a director or is 'employed to invent' he will have the duty to pass on that knowledge to others within the organisation. Other employees do not have to do so unless they wish, which is why many companies run 'suggestion schemes'.

WHAT IS AN EMPLOYEE ENTITLED TO TAKE WITH HIM WHEN HE LEAVES THE COMPANY?

This is best answered by a series of statements:

- He cannot take with him any patents, design rights, copyrights and proprietary information, written or otherwise, which are the property of the company, even if he was the person who created them.

- He can take with him all the other knowhow and skills that he has learnt during his employment with the company.

Proprietary information

This is information (knowhow in other words) that is known to the employee to be valued by the company as an asset of the business. The best way of demonstrating that any information is a valued asset is to identify it by putting it in writing, an example might be the design parameters/considerations for a key item of equipment, and then marking the document as 'confidential – property of xxx Ltd.'.

What use can the employee make of what he can take with him after he has left the company?

Whatever he wishes. He has the right to use his knowledge to earn his living, in whatever way he chooses to do so, unless he is under an obligation not to do so in certain ways. This obligation can come from only one source, a restrictive term in his contract of employment. Any such term will be valid, provided always that it must be reasonable in the circumstances. If it is too restrictive it will be unreasonable.

What is a reasonable clause?

This is difficult, because the law recognises that there are two quite distinct and opposite principles. The company will own confidential knowhow which it wishes to keep secret. The employee, or more correctly the ex-employee, has the right to use his skills to earn his own living. Therefore the company is only allowed to impose a restriction on the freedom of an ex-employee to earn his living where it is completely justifiable for the company to do so. The rules are:

- The company must have an interest to protect – the ex-employee must have had access to valuable information (a salesman to customer details or a design engineer to product details for example).

- The clause must have been accepted by the ex-employee as a part of the terms of his contract of employment.

- The clause must only ask for the minimum that is reasonable to protect the company's interest – if the clause tries too hard it will be invalid and completely ineffective.

A typical clause might be, for a salesperson, 'The employee shall not carry out any work for *any direct competitor* of the employer in any *sales or marketing capacity* within *a particular geographical/market area* for a period of — *months* after this employment contract comes to an end.' The words in italic type in the draft clause must ALL be reasonable. Essentially what the clause is saying is that the company believes that it is reasonable to expect a salesperson not to earn his living after leaving the company by giving a competitor the benefit of his knowledge, until the company has had enough time to put in place an adequately trained successor (and there are lots of other areas for the salesperson to work in).

THE CONSEQUENCES

So if you want to use intellectual property in practice to look after your company, remember what each type gives you. The patent gives you a monopoly on the ideas, but it will only apply to a small proportion of your development work, and it is expensive to obtain and to keep in force. Design rights protect the appearance of products but do not give any protection in relation to what the item does. Design rights and copyrights protect what is drawn or written down, but will not stop anybody borrowing the ideas behind what is written or drawn. Knowhow deals with ideas, but can only be protected by keeping it secret or by using appropriate clauses in contracts. Therefore:

- Consider applying for patents if it seems worthwhile – you can then mark the equipment 'patent applied for' – and the application or patent can always be abandoned if it turns out to be uneconomic.

- Make sure that all drawings and documents are properly marked as the copyright of the organisation, and that drawings are dated and signed by the creator.

- Where appropriate reduce knowhow to writing.

- Mark documents 'confidential' when they contain sensitive information, and most documents do contain sensitive information.

- Don't give information away, except where it is necessary to do so.

- Use contract clauses to put confidentiality obligations in place.

Remember one final thing. Most people and most companies are honest. If they are told that your information is confidential and that you wish them to treat it as confidential they will do so. But if they do not know that it is confidential they will not bother to do so. After all, why should they? The worst mistake, and probably the most common mistake, is to forget to tell people that information actually is confidential.

CHAPTER 15

Forms of Security

Security for payments and performance are always an issue in major contracts, especially when they contain an export/import element. This chapter sets out the basic principles behind the types of security normally used.

ASSETS AS SECURITY

Virtually all forms of security are contract-based, but they fall into two categories: the use of assets as security and the use of third parties as security.

Where assets, and especially land assets, are used as security for loans the lender will require an indemnity agreement allowing him to claim against the assets if the loan and interest are not repaid. Virtually all legal systems require formal registration of this potential claim in one way or another before it can become valid against a third party. This is to prevent the risk of a third party buying the asset without being able to find out that someone already has a claim against it. In the UK, for instance, security against land or buildings will generally be in the form of a 'charge' against the assets which must be registered, usually under the Land Charges Act 1925. (A mortgage is another example of a charge.) The charge may be a fixed charge against a particular asset, or it may be a floating charge, which is a charge against all the assets of a particular type that happen to be owned by the debtor at any time. Banks normally use floating charges as security for overdrafts.

SURETIES AND BONDS

People and companies may act as security either by acting as a 'surety', or by providing a 'bond' of some kind.

SURETIES

A 'surety' is simply a person who undertakes secondary responsibility for the obligations of another person. If B agrees to act as surety for the performance of a contract by A, then A has the primary duty to carry out his contract, but if A does not do so then B will become responsible, either to carry out the contract himself, or to ensure that someone else does so. (Often a 'parent company guarantee' will actually be a surety agreement.)

BONDS

Legally a 'bond' is simply an undertaking that is binding upon the person giving that undertaking because it is done as a deed or under seal.

In this context, however, a bond is a binding undertaking to pay a certain sum of money if called upon to do so. Bonds may be given in different ways, either by a bank in the form of a bank 'guarantee', or by some other organisation, an insurance/finance company for example in the form of what we will call a 'finance company bond'.

A bank guarantee consists of a formal undertaking by the bank to pay a certain sum of money, as stated in the guarantee, upon certain conditions if claimed by the person in whose favour the guarantee has been issued during the validity period of the guarantee. Of course the bank will recover any money that it has to pay out against the guarantee from its own customer, on whose behalf it has issued the guarantee, by deducting that amount from his bank account, or by adding it to his overdraft.

Other financial organisations, merchant banks, insurance and finance companies, and surety companies who provide finance company bonds will normally require some form of indemnity agreement from the company, often in the form of a registered charge on the company's property.

Finance company bonds may well look very like bank guarantees but they tend to operate, though this has been the subject of considerable legal dispute, in a different way to the bank guarantee. A bank will usually pay against a guarantee in full 'on first demand', that is in full as soon as the claim has been made in the appropriate form. Payments under finance company bonds will normally only be made in arrears, after the claimant has incurred expenditure.

Types of bond

Bonds are usually used as a security, either security for the performance of obligations under or in respect of the contract, or for the payment or repayment of sums paid or payable under the contract. Their main use is in export/import contracts, and typically they are used in four contract situations, one relating to the purchaser and three relating to the contractor.

Purchaser bonds

- Occasionally a purchaser, particularly one in a politically or economically difficult country, may be required to provide a bond as security for all payments due under the contract, usually from a national or state bank, as a condition for the provision of cover by the Exports Credit Guarantees Department (see Chapter 16).

Contractor bonds

Contractor bonds can be of three types:

- The contractor may provide a 'bid bond' as security for a tender or bid made to a customer. The bond may then be called in if the contractor seeks to back away from his bid or seek to refuse to accept the contract when offered to him. Typically such a bond might be for 3–5 per cent of the value of the bid.

- The contractor may provide a 'down/progress payment bond' as security for a down payment or progress payment made under the contract, when the contractor has not yet provided value for the payment that he is receiving. The bond might be called in if the contractor failed to deliver the equipment or carry out the work.

- The contractor may provide a 'performance bond' as security for final payments paid in advance before the completion of the defects liability period under the contract. This bond might be called in if the contractor fails to honour their mechanical/performance guarantees under the contract.

The problems with bonds

A bond solves a problem. It provides one side in the contract with financial security for the obligations of the other. Unfortunately, however, a bond, when it is a bank guarantee, is itself a problem as well. It is in simple terms rather like an uncashed cheque. It is always vulnerable to being called in by the holder, even if circumstances do not justify it – what is sometimes called 'unfair calling' of the guarantee. It is also vulnerable to an '*extend* (the validity of the guarantee) *or* (I will) *call* (it in)' threat.

At least if a finance company bond, as opposed to a bank guarantee is called in, the giver of the bond has some protection. It will be necessary for the claimant to prove to the provider of the bond that his claim is at least to some extent justified before money will be paid out. However if a first demand bank guarantee is called then money will be paid without the bank making any real effort to ascertain whether the claim is valid. Even if the claim is invalid the bank will still pay. In the banking world, to this extent at least 'my word is my bond'.

Theoretically at least it is possible to insure, against the unfair calling of a bond. However this cover is very uncertain. Export Credits Guarantees Department, (see Chapter 16) offers insurance cover for export contracts for instance, but their policy can perforce only cover situations where the contractor can show that there are no grounds for calling the bond at all. (And how often in a major contract can any company show that it has complied completely with every single contract requirement?)

In addition there is the problem of the validity of bonds. Under UK law, and most other western European systems, a bond ceases to be valid after the validity period stated within the bond expires, unless specifically extended by the bank or other organisation that has provided the bond. However under some other systems of law, bonds may have a much longer life. Under the law of India, for instance, any bond held in India by any organisation has a life of 20 years from the date of issue. Some other countries, such as Syria, have laws that provide that a bond is valid in perpetuity until returned for cancellation.

However giving a bank guarantee is much less expensive for the contractor than giving a finance company bond which in its turn is infinitely less expensive for the contractor than having the purchaser retain the cash. The cost of a retention is anything up to $1^1/_2$ per cent per month. The cost of a bond is anything up to 5 per cent per year. The cost of a bank guarantee is anything up to 1 per cent per year.

CHAPTER 16

Exporting and Importing

This final chapter deals with some of the more common terms and devices that we can meet when contracts extend beyond one country. Once we understand the rules they are usually easy to deal with.

THE LETTER OF CREDIT

We are all used to the easy ways of paying money to another company, in cash, by cheque and by direct bank-to-bank transfers. They need no comment. But a payment device often used in export/import contracts, the 'letter of credit', or 'documentary credit' as it is also known, can often create difficulties for those not used to working with them.

A letter of credit is an arrangement between two banks. One bank, the 'paying bank', agrees to pay money usually to a contractor, when, and only when, the contractor has satisfied *precisely* the requirements stated in the letter. The other bank, the 'opening bank', which sets up the arrangement at the request of the purchaser, agrees to reimburse that money. Both banks charge fees for their services which are (usually) paid by the purchaser.

Letters of credit are as old as the banking system itself. They evolved as a device to enable merchants to travel without having to carry with them large amounts of heavy and vulnerable money, gold or silver. The merchant would pay his money to a local banker who would give him a letter to carry with him authorising another banker to pay the money back to him (less a commission) once his identity was proved. (As soon as another merchant needed to travel in the opposite direction the two bankers would balance their transactions with each other.)

It now provides a convenient way to pay for exported/imported goods or services. When exporting/importing there is often a significant delay between the goods leaving the control of the contractor and reaching the purchaser. Also the two are in different countries and will often be out of easy direct contact with each other. As a result the contractor may be reluctant to release goods without payment, and the purchaser may be equally reluctant to release payment until he has received goods which meet the contract.

The letter of credit allows the contractor to be paid reasonably quickly. It also enables the purchaser to be reasonably sure that money is not paid until the proper goods are on their way to him and that he will have the right to claim delivery in due course. It does this by concentrating rigidly upon the paperwork.

SETTING UP A LETTER OF CREDIT

This process is straightforward. The purchaser will ask a bank, usually a large national or international bank to set up/open a letter of credit in the name of the contractor and with an appropriate bank in the contractor's country. The opening bank will ask a series of questions of the purchaser (often simply by asking him to fill in a form), and will then set up the letter strictly in accordance with the answers that the purchaser has given. Once set up it is extremely difficult to amend a letter – therefore it is essential to get it correct in the first place. The opening bank will charge an opening and commitment fee to the purchaser, including the fees of the paying bank, and will also want some form of security from the purchaser for payment for the goods by them in due course. The opening bank will then send a document to the paying bank. This document is the letter of credit.

To ensure that it is correct in the first place, simply include a draft text for the letter as an attachment to the contract and then require payment to be made 'by means of a letter of credit in accordance with attachment … to be opened by the buyer with a first-class bank in …'. (A 'first-class' bank simply means a clearing bank.)

Operation

The letter of credit will request the paying bank to pay the amount, or amounts, stated in the letter to the contractor when the contractor has complied with the terms set out within the letter. These terms will usually be that the contractor must deliver to the paying bank during the validity period of the letter a claim for that amount supported by various export/delivery/shipping/inspection and other documents all as listed in the letter. These documents will constitute proof that the correct goods have been properly delivered in accordance with the contract. Once these documents have been handed to the paying bank, the paying bank will transfer the amount(s) due to the contractor, draw down an equivalent amount from the opening bank, and send the documents to the opening bank. The opening bank will then hand the documents to the purchaser when payment is made or arranged by the purchaser in his turn. The purchaser will then use the documents to claim possession of the goods from the carrier or shipper when they arrive at their destination.

Movement of goods, documents and money

To understand the way the letter of credit operates it is best to consider the routes taken by the goods, documents and money:

- The goods and services. The contractor will deliver goods and provide services in accordance with the contract in the normal way. They move from contractor to purchaser.

- The documents. Documents may be of several different kinds:
  - about the goods – such as certificates of origin, and inspection/quality certificates of various kinds;
  - delivery details – such as packing details, packing lists, consignment details;
  - delivery arrangements – such as insurance details, shipping requirements and confirmations; and
  - delivery documents – such as a warehouse receipt, bill of lading, sea or air waybill, road or rail consignment note.

  The documents move from contractor to paying bank, to opening bank, to purchaser. Each movement is matched by payment moving in the opposite direction.

- The money. The money moves by stages, in return for the movement of documents.

Precision and timing

The difficult part is making the correct claim within the correct time period:

- When the contractor has delivered the goods to the carrier or shipper he will submit his claim/invoice to the paying bank. This claim must be in the precise form required by the letter of credit and be accompanied by all the documents necessary, again precisely in accordance with the letter. If they are not precisely in accordance with the letter the paying bank will withhold payment. This means two things:
  - The letter must reflect what is actually going to happen. If, for instance the goods will or may be delivered in more than one consignment, the letter must include the statement 'part shipments and part payments permissible...', or words to that effect. If the letter requires payment documents relating to a single consignment only, then the paying bank can only pay against those payment documents.
  - The documents must reflect *precisely* what is in the letter. This can sometimes result in absurdities, but those are the rules. I myself can remember a contract for 'underwater demolition equipment', in which

my company, because of a typing error in the letter of credit, had to invoice for 'underwear demolition equipment'. The wording was obviously nonsense to ourselves the purchaser and the banks – but the rules are the rules.

- The parties have to decide how to deal with the risk of lateness or delay in delivery. Letters of credit are usually opened for a set validity/claim period. If, due to force majeure or lateness the contractor fails to submit his claim(s) during that validity period, the letter will cease to be valid. In that case it will need to be extended, but this requires agreement by both the purchaser and the contractor, and the payment by one or other of an extension fee to the banks.

THE NEGOTIABLE INSTRUMENT

This is what the banks call 'paper'. It is a document that creates a right to receive money, which can be negotiated, that is bought and sold. When a negotiable instrument is sold or transferred from one person to another it will be endorsed, that is signed, to signify that the transfer of ownership has taken place. When the time for payment arrives whoever then owns the instrument can claim the money. There are three types of negotiable instrument, the 'bill of exchange', the 'promissory note' and certain types of cheque.

BILL OF EXCHANGE

This is a device for making deferred, as opposed to immediate, payments at a distance and also a method of transferring large amounts of money. It is a document by which a party, usually a bank, promises to pay a certain sum of money on a set date to whoever holds that document at that date.

Operation

Suppose I am selling equipment to a purchaser in say Ecuador for a price of £10 million. I agree with the purchaser to accept payment of the price in two instalments, each of £5 million plus interest, one four years and the other five years after delivery. The purchaser will arrange for a bank in Ecuador to make the payments when they fall due. Now I will draw up two bills of exchange for £5 million plus interest, (each about the size of a normal cheque), one payable four and the other five years after the contract delivery date. They will be signed by the Ecuadorian bank, which by doing so accepts the responsibility for payment in due course. The bills will be held in 'escrow' (see below) by a UK bank, and then given to me after the equipment has been delivered. Now I have in my possession two documents worth £10 million plus interest. I can hold on to them and use them to claim payment when they fall due, or I can negotiate them – simply sell them to the bank. If I sell them to the bank I will endorse them, that is sign them on the back, as evidence that I have transferred them to the bank, and the bank will pay me my £10 million. Then the bank can decide whether to hold them or sell them in its turn.

Escrow simply means that something is given to some responsible organisation, in this case the two documents to the bank, with strict instructions to hold it in safe keeping, and to hand it over to someone when certain conditions are satisfied.

THE WORLD SYSTEM

In broad terms the civil law of letters of credit and negotiable instruments is identical to English law. Most civil law countries have statute law dealing with the question (as opposed to dealing with it as a part of the code), and in fact most European laws follow the rules laid down in a Geneva Convention of 1933, an international agreement for the codification of law relating to letters of credit and negotiable instruments. (Virtually all countries in the world have similar law.) There are of course some (very) minor differences here and there, but the letter of credit and the negotiable instrument/bill of exchange are recognised almost universally, for obvious reasons – banking is a worldwide system.

CREDIT RISK INSURANCE

Every major exporting country wishes to encourage exports. One way of doing so is to provide some degree of protection against the particular non-payment risks in export contracts. The agency by which this is done in the UK is the ECGD, the Exports Credit Guarantees Department. Similar organisations exist in many other countries, COFACE in France, Hermes in Germany, the Exim Bank in the USA, NEXI in Japan and so on.

These organisations provide insurance cover for contractors against the risk of non-payment due to the financial failure of an overseas customer or due to political risks, such as a revolution. Cover is subject to approval of the purchaser by the credit agency and to the use by the contractor of normal commercial procedures to ensure payment, (typically for instance asking for payment by a letter of credit). In addition they provide the essential credit risk backing for the financing of projects by bank loans to buyer countries.

SHIPPING TERMS

The world of shipping is full of jargon that needs to be understood. (For instance a 'clean on board FOB bill of lading' means a formal shipping receipt showing that the goods have arrived on the ship with no apparent damage to any of the packing cases within the consignment.)

These terms are used to define the delivery basis. They provide for the point at which the goods are to be delivered by the supplier, and the responsibilities of the contractor and purchaser relating to that delivery. Broadly there are thirteen:

- EXW Ex works – packed ready for collection by the purchaser at a stated location

- FCA Free to a carrier – packed ready for collection and loaded by the contractor on to the carrier's vehicle

- FAS Free alongside a ship – delivered by the contractor to the quayside at the named port for export, and cleared for export

- FOB Free on board a ship – and loaded on to the ship by the contractor as well (note that FOB in American language can mean simply EXW)

- CFR Cost and freight to port of destination – and with shipping cost to destination paid by the contractor as well

- CIF Cost insurance and freight to port of destination – and with marine insurance paid by the contractor as well

- CPT Carriage paid to destination – delivered by the contractor to a carrier with transport costs to destination paid by the contractor as well

- CIP Carriage and insurance paid to destination – and with transport insurance paid by the contractor as well

- DAF Delivered at frontier – ready for unloading from a vehicle and import into the purchaser's country

- DES Delivered ex ship at port of destination – delivered ready for unloading from a ship at the port of import

- DEQ Delivered ex quay at port of destination – and unloaded from the ship

- DDU Delivered duty unpaid at place of destination – still loaded on transport but ready for import

- DDP Delivered duty paid at place of destination – still loaded on transport.

Sometimes local custom and practice can mean that these terms have different local meanings. As a result, one of the great services to international trade by the International Chamber of Commerce over the years has been to publish standard definitions of these terms, which are easy to understand and apply, so avoiding any misunderstanding or dispute. They are published as a book in both English and French, which sets out easy-to-follow definitions of the responsibilities of both contractor and purchaser for each term. The current edition at the time of writing is *Incoterms 2000*. Normal practice would be to state in the contract that the equipment would be delivered, for example 'FOB UK port (Incoterms 2000) ...' and so on. Incoterms should be required reading for any shipping department.

Index